NLT STUDY SERIES
ROMANS

ROMANS

Know the Truth

Douglas J. Moo
Sean A. Harrison
Sean A. Harrison, General Editor

Tyndale House Publishers, Inc.
Carol Stream, Illinois

Visit Tyndale's exciting Web sites at www.nltstudybible.com, www.newlivingtranslation.com, and www.tyndale.com

NLT Study Series: Romans

Designed by Timothy R. Botts and Dean Renninger

Edited by Sean A. Harrison

ISBN 978-1-4143-2198-1 Softcover

Printed in the United States of America

15   14   13   12   11   10   09
7   6   5   4   3   2   1

The purpose of the *NLT Study Series* is to call individuals and groups into serious conversation with God and engagement with his word.

We have designed these studies to provide you and your group with a complete, new Bible study experience. Our aim has been to help you engage seriously with the Bible's content, interacting with it in a meaningful and deeply personal way, not just regurgitating rote answers to fill-in-the-blank questions or producing purely subjective opinions. We also hope to encourage true community study with the honest sharing of different perspectives and experiences. Most of all, we want to help foster your direct communication with God, encouraging you to tell God what is on your mind and heart. We want to help you understand what God is teaching you and apply it to the realities of personal and community life.

To this end, each study in the *NLT Study Series* includes twelve weeks of individual and group studies focusing on understanding the meaning of the text of Scripture, reflecting on it personally and with others, and responding actively to what God is saying to you through it.

Each volume of the *NLT Study Series* can be used by itself, with no other resources, but you can also use it with your Bible of choice. Each volume of the *NLT Study Series* includes, along with the twelve-week study, one book of the *NLT Study Bible*, with both the text of Scripture and all of the study aids alongside it. The *NLT Study Bible* was designed to open up the world of the Bible and to make the meaning and significance of Scripture clear, so it makes a great personal and small-group study resource.

It is our hope and prayer that these studies will help you and those in your group to understand God's word more clearly, to walk with God more fully, and to grow with one another in relationship with our God.

Open my eyes to see
   the wonderful truths in your instructions. PSALM 119:18
Come . . . let us walk in the light of the LORD! ISAIAH 2:5

Sean A. Harrison
General Editor

CONTENTS

INTRODUCTION TO THE
Romans Study

IN ROMANS PAUL EXPLAINS the Good News about Jesus Christ. "It is the power of God at work, saving everyone who believes—the Jew first and also the Gentile" (Rom 1:16). William Tyndale, one of the earliest and greatest English Bible translators, once said that Romans is "a light and a way in unto the whole scripture," and that "the more it is studied the easier it is, the more it is chewed the pleasanter it is, . . . so great treasure of spiritual things lieth hid therein."[1]

Paul addresses a number of questions and problems based on the Good News and its implications. What should we think about the Torah, God's law? What is the status of the Jewish people? What is the role of the Holy Spirit? Should we feel free to eat meat that had been sacrificed to idols and then sold in the public market? As you read, ask how each of the passages is related to "the Good News about Christ" (Rom 1:16). Keeping the Good News in mind as the central theme of the letter will help you understand what Paul is communicating in each of the parts of the letter.

Romans, like all of Paul's writings, is a letter to a specific group of Christians. In the first week of your study, you will read the introduction to Romans from the *NLT Study Bible*. Read it carefully and thoughtfully. Pay close attention to the "Setting," which explains the situation in which Romans was written. Read the "Summary" and "Purpose" sections to form in your mind the big picture of the letter. Then, as you work through the rest of Romans, refer back to the introduction periodically—particularly the "Purpose" and "Summary"—to remind yourself of the big picture and of Paul's purpose in writing the section you are currently studying.

Romans is not easy. There are, certainly, passages that speak directly and clearly. "We know that God causes everything to work together for the good of those who love God," says Paul in Rom 8:28, and we who believe him find encouragement as we go through difficulty. Likewise, we are comforted when we see our own sin for what it is and then read, "There is no condemnation for those who belong to Christ Jesus" (Rom 8:1). Such passages are clear and precious.

Other passages are difficult to grasp, as Paul reasons precisely and methodically in support of his points. This study will challenge you to work through Paul's reasoning and arguments, and it will reward your perseverance.

"To grapple with Romans is to engage in dialogue with one of the most creative theological minds of all time from the most creative period of Christian thought."[2] Wrestle with Paul, seek to grasp what he is saying, and argue with him when you need to. Engage in vigorous dialogue with Paul and with God as you study Romans.

May you find Romans to be "a light and a way," full of precious and great treasure. May God give you a fuller understanding, through Romans, of how the Good News about Christ "is the power of God at work, saving everyone who believes."

Sean A. Harrison
Wheaton, Illinois
April 2009

[1] From the prologue to Romans in the Tyndale New Testament (1534 edition), quoted in F. F. Bruce, *Romans* (Grand Rapids: Eerdmans, 1985), 9.
[2] James D. G. Dunn, *Romans 1–8* (Dallas: Word Books, 1988), xiii.

How to Use This Study

THE PRIMARY WAY we recommend using this Bible study guide is for personal daily meditation and study, along with weekly fellowship and discussion.

The introductory session (p. A13) is designed to launch the group study. Group participants need not prepare for this session, but the leader is encouraged to work through it in advance in order to be able to guide the group effectively. The introductory session provides orientation to the Letter to the Romans, and gives a taste of what the daily and weekly study will be like for the following twelve weeks.

Each week, there are five personal daily studies plus a group session. You can use the daily study guide for your personal daily conversation with God, or you can use it around the table with your family.

You don't need to participate in a weekly group meeting in order to use this study guide. For instance, you can just do the study individually, working through the daily studies and then using the weekly group session as a time of reflection.

Similarly, you don't have to use the study on a daily basis in order to benefit from using it in a group setting. You can just do the study with the group each week by reading the passages, thinking about the discussion questions, and participating in the group discussion.

Ultimately, it's between you and God how you use this study. The more you put into it, the more you will get out of it. If you are meeting with a group, we encourage you to decide together what your level of commitment will be, and then encourage each other to stick with it. Then keep up your part of your commitment to the group.

RECOMMENDATIONS FOR DAILY STUDY

Each daily study is designed to be completed within 15 minutes, but optional "Further Study" is usually provided for those who want to go into greater depth.

Start the daily study by reading the passage recommended for each day. Reflect on what it means, and write down your questions and thoughts about it.

You can use the space provided in the book to write thoughts and answers to questions. If you find that you need more space, we recommend purchasing a small blank book with lined paper to use as a Bible study journal. Use the journal to write your answers to the reflection questions, your own thoughts about the passage, what you think God is saying to you, and your prayers to God about what you have studied.

The NLT Study Series is designed to be used with the *NLT Study Bible*. The letter to the Romans from the *NLT Study Bible* is included for your reading and study. You can also use the *NLT Study Bible* itself, either the print edition or the online version at www.nltstudybible.com. The included section of the *NLT Study Bible* retains its page numbering, so the study guide can be used to refer to either the included section or the *NLT Study Bible* itself.

It can be helpful to highlight or mark the Bible text and study materials where they answer your questions or speak to you in some way. You can:

- underline, circle, or highlight significant words and phrases,
- put brackets around sections of text,
- write keywords in the margin to indicate a topic,
- write page numbers cross-referencing the study guide,
- write dates cross-referencing your journal entries.

Finally, talk with God about what you are learning and how you are responding to it, but also take time to listen to him and hear what he might be saying to you through it. Cultivate your relationship with God day by day.

RECOMMENDATIONS FOR GROUP STUDY

When the group comes together, read the entire passage for the week together, then spend some time letting each person share their own dialogue with God and the Bible that week: insights they've gained, questions they have, and so on.

Then use the discussion questions to stimulate the discussion for that week. You don't have to do all of the questions—you can pick just one.

When the discussion is winding down, spend some time reflecting on what God is saying to you as a group, and how you are going to respond to what God is saying. Spend some time praying together about these things.

Finally, take a look at the passage for the coming week, and make sure everyone understands what they will be doing in preparation for the next meeting of the group.

The Power of God

SESSION GOALS
- Get oriented to the letter to the Romans.
- Discuss what members hope to learn and how we hope to grow in this study.
- Introduce how we are going to be studying together.
- Answer any questions about how to begin.
- Commit ourselves to the Lord and to each other, to participate to the best of our ability.

GETTING ORIENTED TO THE LETTER TO THE ROMANS
Answer the following questions, either individually, or in discussion together with your group.

What do you know about the apostle Paul? Can you recall any events from his life in the Bible?

What do you know about Paul's letter to the Romans? Can you recall any key verses from the book?

What particular issues are you struggling with in your spiritual life?

How do you hope to grow spiritually from your study of the letter to the Romans?

READING: **ROMANS 1:16-17**
Read Rom 1:16-17 aloud; if you're in a group, choose one reader. Read slowly, clearly, thoughtfully. What questions or observations do you have after reading this passage?

STUDY
In what way is the Good News "the power of God at work"? How is this message powerful?

Why does Paul say that the Good News is for "the Jew first and also the Gentile?" (See also 2:9-11.)

What, according to the study note on Rom 1:17, does it mean to be "right in [God's] sight"? How do we obtain this status?

REFLECTION

Are you right in God's sight? How do you know?

What might God be saying to you through Rom 1:16-17?

QUESTIONS

Do you have questions about doing the daily study or preparing for the next meeting?

PRAYER

Take turns praying about this Bible study and the next twelve weeks. You can tell God what your thoughts and questions are, and ask him for his help, strength, insight. You can thank him for this Bible study and for the Bible itself. You can ask him to speak to you and to the others in the group. The leader, in closing, can also commit this study to God.

WEEK

ONE

Good News and Bad

INTRODUCTION;
ROMANS
1:1-32

OUTLINE

DAY **1** ◆ Romans Introduction

READING: **ROMANS INTRODUCTION, pp.** 1888–1892
> Begin with prayer, asking God to give you insight, understanding, and an open heart to listen to and follow his word.

STUDY
> Read the "Setting" (p. 1888). Why do you think it was important for Paul to address the division between Jewish and Gentile Christians?

> Read the "Summary" (pp. 1889–1890). What is the unifying theme of the letter? How does Paul develop this theme throughout the letter?

> Read "Paul's Purpose in Writing" (pp. 1890–1891). What were Paul's purposes in writing Romans?

FURTHER STUDY (Optional)
> Read the "Interpretation" section (pp. 1891–1892). Do the two schools of thought concerning Romans conflict or harmonize? Is one or the other of them right? Neither? Both? Please explain.

REFLECTION
> What questions does the Romans introduction answer for you? What questions does it raise?

> What do you think God is saying to you through your study of the Romans introduction?

PRAYER
    Talk to God about what you have read, any questions or concerns you might have, and what
    you think he might be saying to you today. You can write your prayer here if you wish.

DAY 2 ◆ Romans 1:1-7

READING: **ROMANS 1:1-7**
    Begin with prayer, asking God to give you insight, understanding, and an open heart
    to listen to and follow his word.

STUDY
    What did Paul mean in saying that he was "a slave of Christ Jesus" (1:1)? When and how
    was Paul "chosen by God to be an apostle and sent out to preach his Good News"? Why
    are these claims important for his letter to the Romans?

    Why is it significant that God's Son was "born into King David's family line" (1:3-4)? How
    did Jesus' resurrection show him "to be the Son of God"?

    How do people receive grace and peace from God (1:7)? How does this grace and peace
    change their lives and experiences?

FURTHER STUDY (Optional)
    The Greek word for "called" (klētos), according to the word study dictionary in the NLT
    Study Bible, means "an invitation to someone to accept responsibilities for a particular
    task or a new relationship. God calls/invites the believer to relationship with him or to a
    particular role in his Kingdom." Also read Matt 22:14; Rom 8:28; 11:29; 1 Cor 1:2, 26;
    Eph 1:18; 4:1; 2 Thes 1:11; 2 Tim 1:9; 2 Pet 1:10; Jude 1:1. How do these passages impact
    your understanding of what it means to be called to belong to Jesus Christ?

As described in Rom 1:1-7, what has God done for you?

What do you think God is saying to you personally through Rom 1:1-7?

PRAYER

Talk to God about what you have read, any questions or concerns you might have, and what you think he might be saying to you today. You can write your prayer here if you wish.

DAY 3 ◆ Romans 1:8-17

READING: **ROMANS 1:8-17**

Begin with prayer, asking God to give you insight, understanding, and an open heart to listen to and follow his word.

STUDY

Paul usually includes a thanksgiving and prayer for his readers near the beginning of his letters. In 1:8, about what does he give thanks for the Roman Christians? What does he pray for them?

How would Paul's visiting the Roman Christians encourage each of them (1:10-12)?

What did Paul hope to accomplish with his visit to the Romans (1:13-15)?

How does 1:16-17 fit into the flow of what Paul is saying in ch 1? When Paul says, "For I am not ashamed of this Good News," what in this context would bring him to say that?

FURTHER STUDY (Optional)

The Greek word for "gift" in 1:11 is *charisma*. The definition of this word in the back of the *NLT Study Bible* says, "This noun refers to a gift generously and freely given as an expression of the giver's favor. In the NT, it often refers to spiritual gifts given by God to believers for various purposes within the body of Christ." Also read Rom 12:6; 1 Cor

1:7; 7:7; 12:4, 28; 1 Tim 4:14; 2 Tim 1:6; 1 Pet 4:10. How could Paul give a *charisma* (spiritual gift) to the Roman Christians?

REFLECTION

If Paul were to visit you or your community, what spiritual gift or blessing would he bring to you? How can you receive that same gift or blessing from God now?

What do you think God is saying to you through your study of Rom 1:8-17?

PRAYER

Talk to God about what you have read, any questions or concerns you might have, and what you think he might be saying to you today. You can write your prayer here if you wish.

DAY 4 ◆ Romans 1:18-23

READING: **ROMANS 1:18-23**

Begin with prayer, asking God to give you insight, understanding, and an open heart to listen to and follow his word.

STUDY

According to the study note on Rom 1:18–3:20, Paul "teaches about universal sinfulness" in this section. That sounds like bad news, so why is teaching about universal sinfulness a part of Paul's explanation of the Good News?

Why, according to 1:18-23, is God angry?

According to 1:19-21, what kinds of things do all people know about God? In what sense do all people "know" God (1:21)? In what sense do they *not* "know" God (1:20)?

In what sense does not worshiping God result in foolishness, according to 1:21-23?

The word for "anger" (Greek *orgē*) is defined in the back of the *NLT Study Bible* as follows: "This noun means a strong feeling of displeasure and antagonism, often the response to a standard being violated. This anger can range from an appropriate response of anger against injustice to sinful, selfish anger." Also read Mark 3:5; John 3:36; Rom 2:5, 8; Eph 2:3; 4:31; 5:6; Col 3:8; Rev 6:17; 16:19; 19:15.

What similarities and differences are there between God's anger and human anger?

Read the cross-references on 1:21-23 (Deut 4:15-19; 2 Kgs 17:15; Ps 106:20; Jer 10:14; 1 Cor 1:20; Eph 4:17-18). What do they show you about the connection between worship and wisdom? Between the non-worship of God and foolishness?

REFLECTION

To what extent does Rom 1:18-23 describe you?

What do you think God is saying to you through your study of 1:18-23?

PRAYER

Talk to God about what you have read, any questions or concerns you might have, and what you think he might be saying to you today. You can write your prayer here if you wish.

DAY 5 ◆ Romans 1:24-32

READING: **ROMANS 1:24-32**

Begin with prayer, asking God to give you insight, understanding, and an open heart to listen to and follow his word.

STUDY

According to 1:24-32, what prompted God to abandon these people? What were the results of God's abandoning them?

Read through the list of vices in 1:28-31 and think about how some of these things are expressed in people's lives and in society today. Can you give examples from things you have seen or heard? Have you experienced any of these things in your own life?

FURTHER STUDY (Optional)
Read 1:24-27 and the study note on 1:26. What is Paul's point in discussing homosexual activity?

Paul says that certain people "suffered within themselves the penalty they deserved." Is this overly harsh? Do people deserve to suffer? What do you make of this?

REFLECTION
Are you in any danger of experiencing God's abandonment? Why or why not?

What response or action is Rom 1:24-32 calling you to right now?

PRAYER
Talk to God about what you have read, any questions or concerns you might have, and what you think he might be saying to you today. You can write your prayer here if you wish.

GROUP SESSION

READING: **ROMANS 1:1-32**
Read Rom 1:1-32 together as a group.

DISCUSSION
You can use the following questions to guide what you share in the discussion. Give each person at least one opportunity to share with the others.

What did you learn from Rom 1:1-32? What was one thing that stood out to you as you studied this passage? How did Rom 1:1-32 surprise you? Do you have questions about this passage or the study materials that haven't been answered? What does God seem to be saying to you through what you have studied?

TOPICS FOR DISCUSSION

You can choose from among these topics to generate a discussion among the members of your group, or you can write your thoughts about one or more of these topics if you're studying solo.

1. Having studied the introduction and first chapter of Romans, how would you summarize the Good News message?

2. Describe your own relationship with God: What is your story? What is your status with God? In what ways do you know him?

3. For people like those who are described in Rom 1:18-32, is there any hope? Why or why not?

GROUP REFLECTION

What is God saying to us as a group through Rom 1:1-32?

ACTION

What are we going to do, individually or as a group, in response to what God is saying to us?

PRAYER

How should we pray for each other in response to God's message to us in this passage?

Take turns talking to God about this passage and about what he is saying.

NEXT: **ROMANS 2:1–3:20 (God's Righteous Judgment and All People's Guilt)**

TWO

God's Righteous Judgment and All People's Guilt

ROMANS
2:1–3:20

OUTLINE

DAY **1** ◆ Romans 2:1-11

READING: **ROMANS 2:1-11**
Begin with prayer, asking God to give you insight, understanding, and an open heart to listen to and follow his word.

STUDY
Why was it wrong for Paul's recipients to condemn the people described in 1:18-32? What does it say about their own hearts? What would be better to do instead?

For what reason(s) does God judge? For what reason(s) does God give eternal life?

What does it tell us about God that he exercises both kindness and patience, and anger and judgment? What are the implications for us?

FURTHER STUDY (Optional)
In 2:1, Paul changes his focus from "they" (1:18-32) to "you." Who are the "you" that Paul has in mind here? How are they different from the people of 1:18-32? How are they similar?

How can it be that both judgment and eternal life are "for the Jew first and also for the Gentile" (2:9-10), while at the same time Paul states that "God does not show favoritism" (2:11)?

REFLECTION
Is there a group that you feel is more favored, or should be more favored, by God? Is there a group that you feel is more condemned, or should be more condemned? How does this passage challenge your thinking about that?

What do you think God is saying to you through your study of this passage?

Talk to God about what you have read, any questions or concerns you might have, and what you think he might be saying to you today. You can write your prayer here if you wish.

DAY 2 ◆ Romans 2:12-20

READING: **ROMANS 2:12-20**

Begin with prayer, asking God to give you insight, understanding, and an open heart to listen to and follow his word.

STUDY

According to the study note on 2:12, what does it mean that Gentiles, who "never had God's written law," will be "destroyed" when they sin? On what basis do you think they are destroyed?

On what basis will Jews be judged? How is the Jews' and Gentiles' judgment similar? How is it different?

According to 2:13, what is the means of being made "right with God"?

FURTHER STUDY (Optional)

How do Gentiles know God's law (2:14-15) even though they haven't received the law in written form? What does this imply about their standing before God? What does it imply about the eternal prospects of those who have never heard the Good News of Christ?

Based on 2:17-20, describe what you know about the "special relationship" the Jewish people have had with God. What were they boasting about? What benefits did having this relationship with God give them (see also 9:4-5)? What did it not give them?

REFLECTION

How is the message about judgment in Rom 2:12-20 part of the "Good News" about Christ?

What do you think God is saying to you through your study of Rom 2:12-20?

PRAYER

Talk to God about what you have read, any questions or concerns you might have, and what you think he might be saying to you today. You can write your prayer here if you wish.

DAY 3 ◆ Romans 2:21-29

READING: ROMANS 2:21-29

Begin with prayer, asking God to give you insight, understanding, and an open heart to listen to and follow his word.

STUDY

When Paul says, "Why don't you teach yourself" (2:21), what did he want his readers to do?

Most of us don't have pagan temples in our neighborhoods, but are there ways in which we, like the Jews of the first century, are guilty of figuratively using "items stolen from pagan temples"?

In light of 2:28-29, what is "a true Jew"? What is "true circumcision"?

The note on 2:29 says, "God's Spirit now writes his law on people's hearts (Jer 31:33-34)." What does this imply for what we do and how we live?

FURTHER STUDY (Optional)

What was Isaiah originally saying to Israel when he wrote Isa 52:5? What does Paul mean by using this quotation in the context of Rom 2:24?

What does it mean to seek "praise from God, not from people" (2:29)? How can we seek praise from God more fully?

Is there anything that you personally, or we as a Christian community, are regularly doing that is inconsistent with what we teach? Are there things that we are doing that is resulting in nonbelievers blaspheming the name of God?

What do you think God is saying to you through your study of Rom 2:21-29?

PRAYER
Talk to God about what you have read, any questions or concerns you might have, and what you think he might be saying to you today. You can write your prayer here if you wish.

DAY 4 ◆ Romans 3:1-8

READING: **ROMANS 3:1-8**
Begin with prayer, asking God to give you insight, understanding, and an open heart to listen to and follow his word.

STUDY
According to 3:1-2 and 9:4-5, what is the "advantage of being a Jew"?

How does the unfaithfulness of some of God's people "prove" God's truth and rightness (3:3-4)?

Read 3:5-8. Why is it not unfair for God to "punish us" for our sin if our sin "helps people see how righteous God is"? What is wrong with the line of reasoning that would see God's judgment of sinners as unfair?

FURTHER STUDY (Optional)
Why did Paul need to express the "advantage of being a Jew" at this point in the discourse (3:1-8)? What had he just said that might lead readers to question that advantage? How does affirming that advantage here support the case that Paul is making?

In 3:4 Paul quotes from Ps 51:4. Read Ps 51, then summarize what Ps 51:4 is communicating in that context. What point is Paul making here with this quotation?

REFLECTION

Has God accomplished good in your life through (not just in spite of) sinful choices you have made? Does that mean those choices were themselves good?

What do you think God is saying to you through your study of Rom 3:1-8?

PRAYER

Talk to God about what you have read, any questions or concerns you might have, and what you think he might be saying to you today. You can write your prayer here if you wish.

DAY 5 ◆ Romans 3:9-20

READING: **ROMANS 3:9-20**

Begin with prayer, asking God to give you insight, understanding, and an open heart to listen to and follow his word.

STUDY

In 3:9 Paul summarizes the argument that he has been making in 1:18–3:8. How do the different parts of 1:18–3:8 support the argument that "all people, whether Jews or Gentiles, are under the power of sin"?

In 3:10-18 Paul quotes several OT passages to support his argument. Summarize the message that Paul is communicating through these quotations.

What conclusion does Paul draw from the fact that "the entire world is guilty before God" (3:19-20)?

Read each of the OT passages that is quoted in 3:10-18 in its original setting. Describe whom each passage is talking about and the point that is being made in that OT passage.

*Ps 14:1-3*_____

Ps 53:1-3 _____

Ps 5:9 _____

*Ps 140:3*_____

Ps 10:7 _____

*Isa 59:7-8*_____

Ps 36:1 _____

REFLECTION
In what ways are you "under the power of sin"?

What do you think God is saying to you through your study of Rom 3:9-20?

PRAYER
Talk to God about what you have read, any questions or concerns you might have, and what you think he might be saying to you today. You can write your prayer here if you wish.

GROUP SESSION

READING: **ROMANS 2:1–3:20**
Read Rom 2:1–3:20 together as a group.

DISCUSSION
You can use the following questions to guide what you share in the discussion. Give each person at least one opportunity to share with the others.

What did you learn from Rom 2:1–3:20? What was one thing that stood out to you as you studied this passage? How did Rom 2:1–3:20 surprise you? Do you have questions about this passage or the study materials that haven't been answered? What does God seem to be saying to you through what you have studied?

TOPICS FOR DISCUSSION

You can choose from among these topics to generate a discussion among the members of your group, or you can write your thoughts about one or more of these topics if you're studying solo.

1. Paul makes it clear that God judges sinful people (including those who are professing believers, such as the original recipients of Romans). Is this message of judgment compatible with the Good News of salvation through faith in Christ? Why or why not?

2. In light of 2:12-16, what do you think are the eternal prospects of those who have not heard and responded to the Good News?

3. What are some ways in which believers "dishonor God by breaking" his law, so that "Gentiles blaspheme the name of God" (Rom 2:23-24)? How can we better honor God through the way we live and treat people?

GROUP REFLECTION

What is God saying to us as a group through Rom 2:1–3:20?

ACTION

What are we going to do, individually or as a group, in response to what God is saying to us?

PRAYER

How should we pray for each other in response to God's message to us in this passage?

Take turns talking to God about this passage and about what he is saying.

NEXT: ROMANS 3:21–4:25 (Being Made Right with God by Faith in Jesus Christ)

THREE

Being Made Right with God by Faith in Jesus Christ

ROMANS
3:21–4:25

OUTLINE

DAY **1** ◆ Romans 3:21-26

READING: ROMANS 3:21-26

Begin with prayer, asking God to give you insight, understanding, and an open heart to listen to and follow his word.

STUDY

Read the study note on 3:21-22. How can we be made right with God "without keeping the requirements of the law"? Is it possible for us to be made right with God by keeping the law? Why or why not?

Read the study notes on 3:24 and 3:25. How does Jesus' sacrifice for our sins free us from the penalty of our sins?

FURTHER STUDY (Optional)

The Greek word behind "sacrifice for sin" (*hilastērion*) is defined in the back of the *NLT Study Bible* as "the means by which sins and offenses are forgiven. The result of atonement is mercy and reconciliation between the sinner and the one wronged. . . . Jesus' atoning sacrifice. *Hilastērion* can also mean the 'place of atonement,' referring to the cover of the Ark." Also read Luke 18:13; Heb 2:17; 9:5; 1 Jn 2:2; 4:10.

In what sense is Jesus your "place of atonement"?

Read the article entitled "God's Unified Plan of Salvation," p. 1899. What continuity is there between Jesus and the Old Testament? What discontinuity is there?

REFLECTION

In what ways have you fallen short (3:23)? What situation does this put you in?

What do you think God is saying to you through your study of Rom 3:21-26?

PRAYER

Talk to God about what you have read, any questions or concerns you might have, and what you think he might be saying to you today. You can write your prayer here if you wish.

DAY 2 ◆ Romans 3:27-31

READING: ROMANS 3:27-31

Begin with prayer, asking God to give you insight, understanding, and an open heart to listen to and follow his word.

STUDY

According to 3:27-28, our acquittal from sin and our status of being right with God is not based on obeying the law but on faith. Please summarize in your own words how this is so.

Does this contradict what Paul said earlier in 2:6-11, that God "will judge everyone according to what they have done"? Why or why not?

FURTHER STUDY (Optional)

In 3:31 Paul says, "only when we have faith do we truly fulfill the law." In what sense (if any) should Christians keep the law of Moses?

If true faith fulfills the law, how does this square with the fact that we are no longer "under the requirements of the law" (6:14) now that we relate to God through faith?

REFLECTION

If there is truly only one God, and one way of being made right with him (by faith in Jesus Christ), what does that imply about your interactions with people of different religions and faith traditions?

What do you think God is saying to you through your study of Rom 3:27-31?

Talk to God about what you have read, any questions or concerns you might have, and what you think he might be saying to you today. You can write your prayer here if you wish.

DAY 3 ◆ Romans 4:1-8

READING: **ROMANS 4:1-8**
Begin with prayer, asking God to give you insight, understanding, and an open heart to listen to and follow his word.

STUDY
In 4:1-3, how does Paul establish that Abraham was right with God on the basis of faith, not obedience?

Read the study note on 4:4-5. If right standing with God could be earned, why would that imply that God is indebted to human beings?

Why is it impossible for God to be indebted to us?

FURTHER STUDY (Optional)
In 4:7-8, what point is Paul making by quoting Ps 32:1-2?

The word "joy" (Greek *makarios*) in 4:7, 8 is defined in the *NLT Study Bible* word study dictionary as "a state or condition of joy and happiness. It implies that the blessed person is in favorable, pleasant, and fulfilling circumstances. It can range from emotional joy to a more sedate, virtuous attitude. There is also often an implication that the person is in a right covenant relationship with God." Also read Matt 5:3; Luke 6:20; 11:28; John 20:29; Acts 20:35; Titus 2:13; Jas 1:12; 1 Pet 3:14; Rev 1:3; 22:7.

In what sense do those who are forgiven have "joy" (*makarios*)?

REFLECTION
Have you ever thought or acted in ways that assumed that God was indebted to you? In what ways?

What do you think God is saying to you through your study of Rom 4:1-8?

PRAYER
Talk to God about what you have read, any questions or concerns you might have, and what you think he might be saying to you today. You can write your prayer here if you wish.

DAY 4 ◆ Romans 4:9-15

READING: **ROMANS 4:9-15**

Begin with prayer, asking God to give you insight, understanding, and an open heart to listen to and follow his word.

STUDY

In 4:9-10, how does Paul make the case that the blessing that God gave Abraham is for the Gentiles as well as the Jews? If Abraham was "counted as righteous . . . because of his faith . . . before he was circumcised," what does this suggest about how and when both Gentiles and Jews are also counted as righteous?

If Abraham was not counted as righteous through circumcision (4:11), then what was the purpose of Abraham's circumcision?

Is "God's promise to give the whole earth to Abraham and his descendants" (4:13-14) still applicable to Abraham's children today? Which of Abraham's descendants are recipients of that promise?

FURTHER STUDY (Optional)

The word "father" (Greek *patēr*) in 4:11 is defined in the *NLT Study Bible* word study dictionary as "a male parent, a father. As an extension of this meaning, it can refer to an ancestor, a spiritual leader in a community, a great religious leader from the past (e.g., Abraham), etc. God has revealed himself as the Father of his people." Also read Matt 5:16; 6:9; 7:11; 1 Cor 1:3; 2 Cor 1:3; Eph 1:3; 1 Thes 2:11; 1 Tim 5:1; Heb 12:9; Jas 1:17; 1 Jn 2:13, 23.

What additional insight does this word study give you about Abraham's role as "spiritual father"?

When did God accept you, and on what basis?

What do you think God is saying to you through your study of Rom 4:9-15?

PRAYER

Talk to God about what you have read, any questions or concerns you might have, and what you think he might be saying to you today. You can write your prayer here if you wish.

DAY **5** ◆ Romans 4:16-25

READING: **ROMANS 4:16-25**

Begin with prayer, asking God to give you insight, understanding, and an open heart to listen to and follow his word.

STUDY

Paul speaks of "faith like Abraham's" (4:16) and then goes on to describe it (4:17-21). What was Abraham's faith like?

What situation was Paul probably referring to when he said that "Abraham believed in the God who brings the dead back to life"? (See note on Rom 4:24; see also Heb 11:19.)

In what way was it for our benefit that Abraham was counted as righteous by faith (4:23-25)?

FURTHER STUDY (Optional)

How is it that those who have faith like Abraham's will receive God's promise, "whether or not we live according to the law of Moses" (4:16), if God gives eternal life only "to those who keep on doing good" (2:7)?

In 4:17 Paul quotes Gen 17:5. What had happened in Gen 17 before God made the promise in Gen 17:5? According to Rom 4:17, what does Paul understand this promise to mean?

REFLECTION

What would be the outcome in your life of having faith like Abraham's? What would be the outcome in your community if the people in it had that kind of faith?

What do you think God is saying to you through your study of Rom 4:16-25?

PRAYER

Talk to God about what you have read, any questions or concerns you might have, and what you think he might be saying to you today. You can write your prayer here if you wish.

GROUP SESSION

READING: **ROMANS 3:21–4:25**

Read Rom 3:21–4:25 together as a group.

DISCUSSION

You can use the following questions to guide what you share in the discussion. Give each person at least one opportunity to share with the others.

What did you learn from Rom 3:21–4:25? What was one thing that stood out to you as you studied this passage? How did Rom 3:21–4:25 surprise you? Do you have questions about this passage or the study materials that haven't been answered? What does God seem to be saying to you through what you have studied?

TOPICS FOR DISCUSSION

You can choose from among these topics to generate a discussion among the members of your group, or you can write your thoughts about one or more of these topics if you're studying solo.

1. What are the implications of Paul's teaching that all people, from Abraham to you and me, are accepted on the basis of faith and not what we do?

2. What would your life and your community be like if you and others had faith like Abraham's?

3. If obedience to "the law" is not required in order to be accepted by God, then what is the place of the law in Christians' lives and communities?

GROUP REFLECTION

What is God saying to us as a group through Rom 3:21–4:25?

ACTION

What are we going to do, individually or as a group, in response to what God is saying to us?

PRAYER

How should we pray for each other in response to God's message to us in this passage?

Take turns talking to God about this passage and about what he is saying.

NEXT: ROMANS 5:1–6:14 (Dead to Sin, Alive to God)

Dead to Sin, Alive to God

ROMANS
5:1–6:14

OUTLINE

DAY **1** ◆ Romans 5:1-5

READING: ROMANS 5:1-5

Begin with prayer, asking God to give you insight, understanding, and an open heart to listen to and follow his word.

STUDY

Why is our peace with God a place of "undeserved privilege" (5:2)?

According to 5:3-4, What is the role of "problems and trials" in your relationship with God?

How does the Holy Spirit's presence in our hearts make us confident that God loves us (5:5)?

FURTHER STUDY (Optional)

The word for "peace" (Greek *eirēnē*) in 5:1 is defined in the *NLT Study Bible* word study dictionary as "a state of concord, peace, and harmony among parties. There is no necessary implication of a previous state of discord. The word can also signify an internal sense of well-being. It often refers to the peace between God and human beings made possible through Christ." Also read Matt 10:34; Luke 2:14; John 14:27; Acts 10:36; Rom 8:6; 14:19; 1 Cor 14:33; Gal 5:22; Eph 2:14; Phil 4:7, 9; Col 3:15; Heb 12:14; 1 Pet 3:11.

What does it mean that those who have faith have "peace with God because of what Jesus Christ our Lord has done for us" (5:1)?

Read the passages listed in the note on 5:3-4 (Jas 1:2-4 and 1 Pet 1:6-7). What are these three passages all teaching?

REFLECTION

Do problems and trials strengthen your "confident hope of salvation"? Why or why not?

What do you think God is saying to you through your study of Rom 5:1-5?

PRAYER

Talk to God about what you have read, any questions or concerns you might have, and what you think he might be saying to you today. You can write your prayer here if you wish.

DAY 2 ◆ Romans 5:6-11

READING: **ROMANS 5:6-11**

Begin with prayer, asking God to give you insight, understanding, and an open heart to listen to and follow his word.

STUDY

In what sense were we helpless before Christ came (5:6)?

In light of 5:7, why is it so remarkable that God sent Christ to die for us "while we were still sinners" (5:8)?

In 5:9, how does the blood of Christ make us "right in God's sight"? How does it guarantee that we will be saved "from God's condemnation"?

FURTHER STUDY (Optional)

The word "made us friends" (Greek *katallagē*) in 5:11 is defined in the *NLT Study Bible* word study dictionary as "the reestablishment of a friendly relationship after it had been seriously disrupted or broken. There is a focus on the change in the relationship from a negative to a positive condition." Also read Rom 11:15; 1 Cor 7:11; 2 Cor 5:18, 19, 20.

What does it mean to have "friendship with God" (5:10)?

REFLECTION

Does your life express the fact that you have a friendship with God? If so, how do you experience that relationship? If not, what is needed for you to have that relationship?

What do you think God is saying to you through your study of Rom 5:6-11?

Talk to God about what you have read, any questions or concerns you might have, and what you think he might be saying to you today. You can write your prayer here if you wish.

DAY 3 ◆ Romans 5:12-19

READING: ROMANS 5:12-19

Begin with prayer, asking God to give you insight, understanding, and an open heart to listen to and follow his word.

STUDY

Did Adam's sin (5:12) make all his descendants already sinful at birth? Or did his sin give us a propensity to sin? Or did his sin affect us in some other manner?

Read the two quotations in the study note on 5:12, both taken from 2 Baruch, a Jewish book that is not in the Hebrew Bible. Which of these two perspectives on the relationship between Adam's sin and ours seems correct to you? Why? Or can you see a way in which they are both true? If so, how?

In light of 5:15-19, if it is true that all people are condemned to death through Adam's sin, is it also true that all people receive "God's gracious gift" of forgiveness and new life in Christ? Please explain.

FURTHER STUDY (Optional)

Read "The Old Realm and the New (5:12–8:39)," p. 1903. How would you describe the two realms? How are they similar? How are they different?

REFLECTION

Is your current standing with God based on Adam's "one sin" that "brings condemnation," or is it based on on Christ's "one act of righteousness" that "brings a right relationship with God and new life"?

What do you think God is saying to you through your study of Rom 5:12-19?

PRAYER

Talk to God about what you have read, any questions or concerns you might have, and what you think he might be saying to you today. You can write your prayer here if you wish.

DAY 4 ◆ Romans 5:20–6:4

READING: **ROMANS 5:20–6:4**

Begin with prayer, asking God to give you insight, understanding, and an open heart to listen to and follow his word.

STUDY

What reason does Paul give in 5:20 for why the law was given to ancient Israel? How does this contrast with what many Jews thought (see study note on 5:20)?

What does Paul mean when he says that "grace rules instead" of sin (5:21)?

In light of 6:1-3, why shouldn't we go ahead and sin if God's grace is guaranteed?

What does it mean to say that those who have been joined with Christ Jesus have died to sin (6:2)?

If someone keeps on sinning freely, does that suggest that person is not joined with Christ? Why or why not?

FURTHER STUDY (Optional)

Read "God's Grace (5:15-17, 20-21)," p. 1901. How would you define God's grace? How does his grace relate to our salvation?

Read through the other passages in Romans that are listed in the first sentence of the theme note (Rom 3:24; 4:4-5, 16; 5:2, 15-21; 6:14-15; 11:5-6) and summarize what they teach us about God's grace.

REFLECTION

What are the implications of the fact that grace now rules our lives?

In what ways have you experienced death and new life in Christ?

What do you think God is saying to you through your study of Rom 5:20–6:4?

PRAYER

Talk to God about what you have read, any questions or concerns you might have, and what you think he might be saying to you today. You can write your prayer here if you wish.

DAY 5 ✦ Romans 6:5-14

READING: ROMANS 6:5-14

Begin with prayer, asking God to give you insight, understanding, and an open heart to listen to and follow his word.

STUDY

Read the study note on 6:6. What are our "old sinful selves"? In what sense were we "slaves to sin" before?

In what sense have we "died with Christ" (6:7)?

What does it mean that we have been "set free from the power of sin" (6:7) and are now "dead to the power of sin" (6:11)?

FURTHER STUDY (Optional)
Read the study note on 6:10. How did Christ's death break the power of sin?

Read the study note on 6:14. What does it mean that we no longer live under the requirements of the law and now live under the freedom of God's grace?

REFLECTION
What changes is God calling you to make in light of your freedom from the power of sin and your new life for the glory of God? In what ways is God calling you to give yourself more fully to him?

What do you think God is saying to you through your study of Rom 6:5-14?

PRAYER
Talk to God about what you have read, any questions or concerns you might have, and what you think he might be saying to you today. You can write your prayer here if you wish.

GROUP SESSION

READING: **ROMANS 5:1–6:14**
Read Rom 5:1–6:14 together as a group.

DISCUSSION
You can use the following questions to guide what you share in the discussion. Give each person at least one opportunity to share with the others.

What did you learn from Rom 5:1–6:14? What was one thing that stood out to you as you studied this passage? How did Rom 5:1–6:14 surprise you? Do you have questions about this passage or the study materials that haven't been answered? What does God seem to be saying to you through what you have studied?

TOPICS FOR DISCUSSION

You can choose from among these topics to generate a discussion among the members of your group, or you can write your thoughts about one or more of these topics if you're studying solo.

1. Paul indicates that peace, hope, and joy are outcomes of faith in Jesus Christ. How have you experienced those blessings in your own life? Or, in what ways does your experience lack those blessings?

2. What does "friendship with God" (5:10, 11) mean for you? What are the practical, daily outworkings of having a personal relationship with God?

3. How does your community or the world in which you live show evidence of a broken relationship, or lack of relationship, with God? What can you and your community do to help cultivate new and growing relationships between people and God?

4. What does it mean for you and your community that believers are "dead to the power of sin and alive to God through Christ Jesus" (6:11)?

GROUP REFLECTION

What is God saying to us as a group through Rom 5:1–6:14?

ACTION

What are we going to do, individually or as a group, in response to what God is saying to us?

PRAYER

How should we pray for each other in response to God's message to us in this passage?

Take turns talking to God about this passage and about what he is saying.

NEXT: ROMANS 6:15–7:25 (Freedom from Sin's Power and the Law's Judgment)

Freedom from Sin's Power and the Law's Judgment

ROMANS
6:15–7:25

OUTLINE

DAY **1** ◆ Romans 6:15-23

READING: ROMANS 6:15-23

Begin with prayer, asking God to give you insight, understanding, and an open heart to listen to and follow his word.

STUDY

If God's grace has freed us from the law, why should we not "go on sinning" (6:15-16)?

What is the result of letting ourselves be "slaves to sin" (6:19-23)?

What does it mean to be slaves to "righteous living" (6:16, 18)?

FURTHER STUDY (Optional)

Read the study note on 6:21 and the passages listed in it, then summarize your understanding of what Paul teaches about eternal death in Romans.

The word translated "holy" and "holiness" (Greek *hagiasmos*) in 6:19, 22 is defined in the *NLT Study Bible* word study dictionary as "dedication to God, both in faithfulness to him and in active service. There is a sense of process toward godliness, with *hagiasmos* being the goal and the result, which is possible through the work of Jesus and his Spirit." Also read 1 Cor 1:30; 1 Thes 4:3, 4, 7; 2 Thes 2:13; 1 Tim 2:15; Heb 12:14; 1 Pet 1:2.

How does righteous living result in our becoming "holy"?

REFLECTION

What would a dedication to avoid sin and live for God look like in your own life?

What do you think God is saying to you through your study of Rom 6:15-23?

Talk to God about what you have read, any questions or concerns you might have, and what you think he might be saying to you today. You can write your prayer here if you wish.

DAY 2 ◆ Romans 7:1-6

READING: ROMANS 7:1-6
Begin with prayer, asking God to give you insight, understanding, and an open heart to listen to and follow his word.

STUDY
In 7:1-3, Paul takes as given that marriage is binding until death. Why is it "committing adultery" to remarry while one's former spouse is still alive? Why is it not adultery if the other person has died?

In 7:4-6, Paul uses the release from the obligation of marriage when one's spouse dies to support his argument that we have been released from our obligation to "the power of the law." What obligation have we been released from? What are the implications of that release?

What does serving God "in the new way of living in the Spirit" mean?

FURTHER STUDY (Optional)
The "power of the law" is a strange turn of phrase. What do you think Paul means by it?

In what sense have we "died" to the power of the law by having "died with Christ"?

REFLECTION
What would it look like in your life to serve God in the new way of living in the Spirit?

What do you think God is saying to you through your study of Rom 7:1-6?

Talk to God about what you have read, any questions or concerns you might have, and what you think he might be saying to you today. You can write your prayer here if you wish.

DAY 3 ◆ Romans 7:7-12

READING: **ROMANS 7:7-12**
Begin with prayer, asking God to give you insight, understanding, and an open heart to listen to and follow his word.

STUDY
What was the original context of God's command, "You must not covet" (7:7)? What is Paul's point in using it as an example?

Read the study note on 7:8. How does sin make use of the law in our hearts?

Read the study notes on 7:9 and 7:10. Why does learning the law result in death?

FURTHER STUDY (Optional)
When Paul wrote in 7:10 that the law's commands "were supposed to bring life," he might have been thinking of passages like Lev 18:1-5. Read this passage and summarize what God was saying to Israel through it.

If this was God's intention for the law, why doesn't the law do what it was supposed to do?

What does Paul mean in saying, "the law itself is holy . . . and right and good" (7:12)?

REFLECTION
What function(s) does the law of God still provide in our lives as believers?

What do you think God is saying to you through your study of Rom 7:7-12?

PRAYER

Talk to God about what you have read, any questions or concerns you might have, and what you think he might be saying to you today. You can write your prayer here if you wish.

DAY 4 ◆ Romans 7:13-17

READING: **ROMANS 7:13-17**

Begin with prayer, asking God to give you insight, understanding, and an open heart to listen to and follow his word.

STUDY

Why is the law not the cause of our spiritual "death" (7:13)? Why might we think that it is?

In what sense are we still slaves to sin (7:14-16)? How can this be true in light of ch 6?

FURTHER STUDY (Optional)

Read "The Limitations of Law (7:1-25)," p. 1905. Summarize in your own words the value and usefulness of God's law, and its limitations.

REFLECTION

Does Paul's description of the believer's struggle with sin match your own experience? If so, how? If not, why do you think it's different?

What do you think God is saying to you through your study of Rom 7:13-17?

PRAYER

Talk to God about what you have read, any questions or concerns you might have, and what you think he might be saying to you today. You can write your prayer here if you wish.

DAY 5 ◆ Romans 7:18-25

READING: **ROMANS 7:18-25**

Begin with prayer, asking God to give you insight, understanding, and an open heart to listen to and follow his word.

STUDY

What is the power living inside believers that makes them do wrong (7:23)?

Among the early Christian churches some had the view that a believer was free to do anything physical, because it was one's body doing it, not one's real identity. Does Paul in this passage show that he holds that viewpoint? Why or why not?

FURTHER STUDY (Optional)

Along with this passage, read the study note on 7:17. Is Paul shirking responsibility for his sin? (Do you find the explanation in the study note convincing?) Why or why not?

REFLECTION

How can a follower of Jesus respond properly to this struggle with sin? Should we just resign ourselves? Or should we fight against it, even though it's a hopeless struggle? Or do we have reason for hoping to overcome sin? If so, how do we go about achieving victory?

What do you think God is saying to you through your study of Rom 7:18-25?

PRAYER

Talk to God about what you have read, any questions or concerns you might have, and what you think he might be saying to you today. You can write your prayer here if you wish.

GROUP SESSION

READING: **ROMANS 6:15–7:25**
Read Rom 6:15–7:25 together as a group.

DISCUSSION

You can use the following questions to guide what you share in the discussion. Give each person at least one opportunity to share with the others.

What did you learn from Rom 6:15–7:25? What was one thing that stood out to you as you studied this passage? How did Rom 6:15–7:25 surprise you? Do you have questions about this passage or the study materials that haven't been answered? What does God seem to be saying to you through what you have studied?

TOPICS FOR DISCUSSION

You can choose from among these topics to generate a discussion among the members of your group, or you can write your thoughts about one or more of these topics if you're studying solo.

1. What function(s) does the law of God still provide in our lives as believers?

2. How can we have "died to sin" (6:2) and be "slaves of God" (6:22) and "slaves to righteous living" (6:18, 19) if, as Paul laments, "I am all too human, a slave to sin" (7:14)? Is Paul's call to personal holiness in ch 6 unrealistic in light of ch 7, or is there a solution?

3. What does your struggle against sin look like? What kinds of situations typically bring failure? When do you experience victory?

GROUP REFLECTION
What is God saying to us as a group through Rom 6:15–7:25?

ACTION
What are we going to do, individually or as a group, in response to what God is saying to us?

PRAYER
How should we pray for each other in response to God's message to us in this passage?

Take turns talking to God about this passage and about what he is saying.

NEXT: **ROMANS 8:1-39 (Eternal Life and Fellowship with God in the Spirit)**

Eternal Life and Fellowship with God in the Spirit

ROMANS
8:1-39

OUTLINE

DAY **1** ◆ Romans 8:1-4

READING: **ROMANS 8:1-4**

> Begin with prayer, asking God to give you insight, understanding, and an open heart to listen to and follow his word.

STUDY

> What does Paul mean when he says that there is "no condemnation for those who belong to Christ Jesus"? On what basis does he say this? (See the study note on 8:1 and also the study note on 8:3, after "a sacrifice for our sins.")

> In what sense have we been freed by "the power of the life-giving Spirit" from "the power of sin that leads to death" (8:2)?

> Is Paul contradicting what he said in ch 7 about our ongoing propensity to sin? Why or why not?

FURTHER STUDY (Optional)

> How was Jesus' body "like the body we sinners have" (see 8:3 and study note)? How was it different? Was Jesus fully "one of us"? Please explain.

> The word translated "sinful nature" (Greek *sarx*, "flesh") in 8:4 is defined in the *NLT Study Bible* word study dictionary as "the entire physical body or simply human existence in general. It sometimes means the external parts of human life, only those that can be observed directly without reference to internal or spiritual realities. Still another meaning is the reasoning, appetites, and desires that relate to the sinful nature, at odds with our redeemed life in God." Also read Matt 16:17; 26:41; John 1:14; 3:6; 1 Cor 5:5; Gal 3:3; 5:19, 24; Eph 5:29; Heb 5:7.

> If *sarx* can mean both our physical bodies and the human sinful nature, does this mean that our physical existence is inherently evil? Why or why not?

REFLECTION

To what extent does your experience reflect Rom 7:15-19 (doing sinful things that I don't want to do), and to what extent does your experience reflect Rom 8:2-4 (no longer following the sinful nature)?

What is the impact of knowing that there is no possibility of condemnation if you belong to Christ Jesus?

What do you think God is saying to you through your study of Rom 8:1-4?

PRAYER

Talk to God about what you have read, any questions or concerns you might have, and what you think he might be saying to you today. You can write your prayer here if you wish.

DAY 2 ◆ Romans 8:5-13

READING: **ROMANS 8:5-13**

Begin with prayer, asking God to give you insight, understanding, and an open heart to listen to and follow his word.

STUDY

What does it mean to be "dominated by the sinful nature" (8:5-9 and study notes)? What does it mean to be "controlled by the Holy Spirit"? How would you describe the contrast between the two situations?

Are believers (those who trust in God for salvation through Jesus Christ and have a personal relationship with God by faith) ever controlled by the sinful nature? Are they always controlled by the Holy Spirit? What is your understanding about this?

Read the study note on 8:13. In what sense does sin bring death? Does this warning apply to believers in Jesus? Why or why not?

Read the study note on 8:6, and review the word study on "peace "(*eirēnē*) that you did in 5:1-5 (p. A40). What sort of peace do you have if you let "the Spirit control your mind"?

Read the study notes on 8:10 and 8:11. In what sense does the Holy Spirit make us alive in our mortal bodies in this life, and in what sense will the Spirit make us alive for eternity?

REFLECTION

Are you being controlled by the sinful nature, or do you have the Spirit of God living in you? In what ways is this situation expressed in your life?

What do you think God is saying to you through your study of Rom 8:5-13?

PRAYER

Talk to God about what you have read, any questions or concerns you might have, and what you think he might be saying to you today. You can write your prayer here if you wish.

DAY 3 ◆ Romans 8:14-22

READING: **ROMANS 8:14-22**

Begin with prayer, asking God to give you insight, understanding, and an open heart to listen to and follow his word.

STUDY

What is the significance of believers' status as "children" of God as opposed to "slaves" (8:14-17 and notes)?

Read the OT references in the note on 8:14. What did it mean for Israel that they were "children of God"?

What are the "pains of childbirth" in which the creation groans (8:22)? What is creation hoping for in the future?

FURTHER STUDY (Optional)

Read the study note on 8:15. The word translated "adopted as his children" (Greek *huiothesia*) is defined in the *NLT Study Bible* word study dictionary as "adoption, with an emphasis that the child has full inheritance rights and the same status as a natural child." Also read Rom 8:23; 9:4; Gal 4:5; Eph 1:5.

In light of this, what is the significance of our being "adopted as his children"?

The word translated "heir" (Greek *sunklēronomos*) in 8:17 is defined in the *NLT Study Bible* word study dictionary as "a person [who] inherits something along with someone else, often with the sense that the coheir is included as a gracious gift. The second party is a full participant in the inheritance, receiving the same benefit as the original heir." Also read Eph 3:6; Heb 11:9; 1 Pet 3:7.

What does it mean that we are, with Christ, "heirs of God's glory"?

REFLECTION

What does it mean to you that God is (or can be) your "Daddy"?

What do you think God is saying to you through your study of Rom 8:14-22?

PRAYER

Talk to God about what you have read, any questions or concerns you might have, and what you think he might be saying to you today. You can write your prayer here if you wish.

DAY 4 ◆ Romans 8:23-30

READING: **ROMANS 8:23-30**

Begin with prayer, asking God to give you insight, understanding, and an open heart to listen to and follow his word.

STUDY

How does this section continue and support Paul's message begun in 8:18, that "what we suffer now is nothing compared to the glory he will reveal to us later"?

In what ways do "we believers also groan" in this life (8:23 and study note)?

According to 8:23-27, how does the Holy Spirit help us? What does it mean that "the Holy Spirit within us" is "a foretaste of future glory"?

FURTHER STUDY (Optional)

How does 8:28-30 support the message that we can have confidence as we hope for what God has in store for us (8:23-27), because nothing can ever separate us from God's love (8:31-39)?

In 8:29-30, who are those that God has "called" and "chosen"? What does it mean that "God knew his people in advance"? Does this passage teach that God saves only those individuals whom he chose in advance to save? Why or why not?

REFLECTION

How have you experienced the help of the Holy Spirit?

In your experience, does everything in your life work together for good in some way? Please explain.

What do you think God is saying to you through your study of Rom 8:23-30?

PRAYER

Talk to God about what you have read, any questions or concerns you might have, and what you think he might be saying to you today. You can write your prayer here if you wish.

DAY 5 ◆ Romans 8:31-39

READING: **ROMANS 8:31-39**
Begin with prayer, asking God to give you insight, understanding, and an open heart to listen to and follow his word.

STUDY
What, in a nutshell, are the "wonderful things" (8:31) that Paul has been saying?

Is Paul saying in 8:31-34 that Christians experience no opposition in this world? What *is* he saying?

How can it be an "overwhelming victory" (8:37) if we are experiencing hardship?

FURTHER STUDY (Optional)
In light of 8:35-36, what is the meaning, for followers of Jesus, of the difficulties that they experience?

REFLECTION
What kinds of things in your life threaten to separate you from God's love. How do you respond to these things? Does this passage suggest you should respond any differently?

What do you think God is saying to you through your study of Rom 8:31-39?

PRAYER
Talk to God about what you have read, any questions or concerns you might have, and what you think he might be saying to you today. You can write your prayer here if you wish.

GROUP SESSION

READING: **ROMANS 8:1-39**
Read Rom 8:1-39 together as a group.

DISCUSSION

You can use the following questions to guide what you share in the discussion. Give each person at least one opportunity to share with the others.

What did you learn from Rom 8:1-39? What was one thing that stood out to you as you studied this passage? How did Rom 8:1-39 surprise you? Do you have questions about this passage or the study materials that haven't been answered? What does God seem to be saying to you through what you have studied?

TOPICS FOR DISCUSSION

You can choose from among these topics to generate a discussion among the members of your group, or you can write your thoughts about one or more of these topics if you're studying solo.

1. Does life in the Spirit (ch 8) provide a solution for the problem of continuing slavery to sin (ch 7)? Why or why not?

2. What are the possibilities and limitations of life in the Spirit? What are the implications for our daily lives that God's Spirit is with us and living in us if we are believers in Christ?

3. In Rom 8, Paul proclaims no condemnation for those who are God's people through Christ, no separation from God's love, a life of power in God's Spirit, and the assurance that God's purposes are being fulfilled. How can we experience the full impact of this message in our lives? How can we more fully express the reality of this message to those around us?

GROUP REFLECTION

What is God saying to us as a group through Rom 8:1-39?

ACTION

What are we going to do, individually or as a group, in response to what God is saying to us?

PRAYER

How should we pray for each other in response to God's message to us in this passage?

Take turns talking to God about this passage and about what he is saying.

NEXT: **ROMANS 9:1-29 (God's Chosen People)**

*God's Chosen
People*

ROMANS
9:1-29

OUTLINE

DAY **1** ◆ Romans 9:1-5

READING: **ROMANS 9:1-5**
> Begin with prayer, asking God to give you insight, understanding, and an open heart to listen to and follow his word.

STUDY
> Read the study note on Rom 9:1–11:36. What problem is Paul addressing in this section, and why is it a problem? What solution to the problem does Paul give?

> Read the passages listed in the study note on 9:3 (Lev 27:28-29; Josh 6:17-18; 7:1, 11-13; 22:20; 1 Sam 15:3; 1 Chr 2:7). What did Paul mean when he said that he was willing to be *anathema*?

> What is the significance of saying "Christ himself was an Israelite as far as his human nature is concerned" (9:5)?

FURTHER STUDY (Optional)
> Read the study note on 9:4, along with Exod 4:22; Jer 3:19; 31:9; and Hos 11:1. In these passages, what is the significance of Israel's being the "son" or "child" of God, their "Father"?

REFLECTION
> Is there anyone that you care for so much that you would be willing to go to hell to save them? Since that is not a feasible proposition, what *can* you do for their salvation? How can you pray for those you care about?

> What do you think God is saying to you through your study of Rom 9:1-5?

PRAYER

Talk to God about what you have read, any questions or concerns you might have, and what you think he might be saying to you today. You can write your prayer here if you wish.

DAY **2** ◆ Romans 9:5-24

READING: **ROMANS 9:5-24; "GOD IS IN CHARGE"**

Read Rom 9:5-24 and the article, "God Is in Charge," p. 1909.

Begin with prayer, asking God to give you insight, understanding, and an open heart to listen to and follow his word.

STUDY

The article states that "in Rom 9, Paul shows that God determines the course of salvation." How does he do so?

What is your understanding of the role of God's action and the role of human decision in salvation?

FURTHER STUDY (Optional)

Read some of the passages listed in the margin next to the article. What do these passages teach you about God's sovereign rule over the world?

REFLECTION

What does it mean for you that God is in charge?

What do you think God is saying to you through your study of Rom 9:5-24?

Talk to God about what you have read, any questions or concerns you might have, and what you think he might be saying to you today. You can write your prayer here if you wish.

DAY 3 ◆ Romans 9:6-13

READING: ROMANS 9:6-13

Begin with prayer, asking God to give you insight, understanding, and an open heart to listen to and follow his word.

STUDY

Why does Paul in 9:6 raise the question of whether God has "failed to fulfill his promise to Israel"?

What answer to the question does Paul provide in this section? How does he support his answer?

In 9:7-9, what point is Paul making by discussing Isaac as the only one of Abraham's children who was "counted" as Abraham's descendant?

Who, then, are "the children of the promise" that "are considered to be Abraham's children"?

FURTHER STUDY (Optional)

What argument is Paul making in 9:10-13? What is his point in making this argument here?

REFLECTION

Are you one of Abraham's "children of promise" (9:8)? Why or why not?

What do you think God is saying to you through your study of Rom 9:6-13?

Talk to God about what you have read, any questions or concerns you might have, and what you think he might be saying to you today. You can write your prayer here if you wish.

DAY 4 ◆ Romans 9:14-23

READING: **ROMANS 9:14-23**
Begin with prayer, asking God to give you insight, understanding, and an open heart to listen to and follow his word.

STUDY
Read the study notes on 9:14-16 and 9:15. What has Paul said that would lead some people to conclude that God is unfair? Why was God not being unfair?

How does the example of Pharaoh in 9:17-18 support Paul's point?

How does God's patience toward "those on whom his anger falls . . . make the riches of his glory shine even brighter"?

FURTHER STUDY (Optional)
What point is Paul making with his quotation in 9:15 of Exod 33:19?

Read Isa 29:16; 45:9-10. What is the message of these passages?

REFLECTION
What are the implications of God's lack of obligation in relationship to his creation?

What do you think God is saying to you through your study of Rom 9:14-23?

PRAYER

Talk to God about what you have read, any questions or concerns you might have, and what you think he might be saying to you today. You can write your prayer here if you wish.

DAY 5 ◆ Romans 9:24-29

READING: **ROMANS 9:24-29**

Begin with prayer, asking God to give you insight, understanding, and an open heart to listen to and follow his word.

STUDY

In Rom 9:25-26, Paul quotes Hos 2:23 and 1:10. About whom was God speaking in Hosea's original prophecy? How do these prophecies apply to Gentiles?

In 9:27-29, Paul quotes Isa 10:22-23 and 1:9. What was God originally saying to the people of Israel through these passages?

How do these quotations from Hosea and Isaiah support Paul's point, that believers are God's chosen people, "both from the Jews and from the Gentiles" (9:24)?

REFLECTION

According to this passage, God has chosen people from all nations to be his people. What does this tell you about God? What is your response?

What do you think God is saying to you through your study of Rom 9:24-29?

PRAYER

Talk to God about what you have read, any questions or concerns you might have, and what you think he might be saying to you today. You can write your prayer here if you wish.

GROUP SESSION

READING: **ROMANS 9:1-29**

Read Rom 9:1-29 together as a group.

DISCUSSION

You can use the following questions to guide what you share in the discussion. Give each person at least one opportunity to share with the others.

What did you learn from Rom 9:1-29? What was one thing that stood out to you as you studied this passage? How did Rom 9:1-29 surprise you? Do you have questions about this passage or the study materials that haven't been answered? What does God seem to be saying to you through what you have studied?

TOPICS FOR DISCUSSION

You can choose from among these topics to generate a discussion among the members of your group, or you can write your thoughts about one or more of these topics if you're studying solo.

1. Paul was willing to go to hell if it would save his fellow countrymen. Whom do you care about deeply and would do just about anything to save? What *can* you do for them?

2. In Rom 9 Paul presents God as free to choose whom he will for blessing and for destruction. What are the implications of this portrayal of God? Are you comfortable with this portrayal? Why or why not?

3. Paul makes it clear in Rom 9 that God chooses people from every nation to belong to his people. Have you or others you know ever had trouble treating people from another group fully as "children of the living God" (9:26)? What is one practical thing that you or your community can do to break down these walls?

GROUP REFLECTION

What is God saying to us as a group through Rom 9:1-29?

ACTION

What are we going to do, individually or as a group, in response to what God is saying to us?

PRAYER

How should we pray for each other in response to God's message to us in this passage?

Take turns talking to God about this passage and about what he is saying.

NEXT: ROMANS 9:30–10:21 (Christ as the Climax of Salvation History)

*Christ as the
Climax of Salvation
History*

ROMANS
9:30–10:21

OUTLINE

DAY **1** ◆ Romans 9:30-33

READING: **ROMANS 9:30-33**
> Begin with prayer, asking God to give you insight, understanding, and an open heart to listen to and follow his word.

STUDY
> Why does God accept the Gentiles even though they "were not trying to follow God's standards"?

> Why did Israel not succeed in getting "right with God by keeping the law"? What motivated Israel to use that approach?

> What does it mean that Israel "stumbled over the great rock"? Why did that happen?

FURTHER STUDY (Optional)
> The word translated "stumble" (Greek *proskomma*) in 9:32-33 is defined in the *NLT Study Bible* word study dictionary as "an object that trips a person." Also read Matt 5:29; 16:23; 18:6; Rom 14:13, 20; 1 Cor 1:23; 8:9, 13; Gal 5:11; 1 Pet 2:8. How does "the rock" make people stumble?

REFLECTION
> Have you seen examples in your own experience of people stumbling over Christ? What happened?

> What do you think God is saying to you through your study of Rom 9:30-33?

PRAYER

Talk to God about what you have read, any questions or concerns you might have, and what you think he might be saying to you today. You can write your prayer here if you wish.

DAY 2 ◆ Romans 10:1-4

READING: **ROMANS 10:1-4**

Begin with prayer, asking God to give you insight, understanding, and an open heart to listen to and follow his word.

STUDY

At the time of Paul, how were the people of Israel expressing their enthusiasm for God? Why was this "misdirected zeal"?

What is "God's way of making people right with himself"?

How has "Christ . . . already accomplished the purpose for which the law was given"?

REFLECTION

Have you ever expressed misdirected zeal for God or something else? Have you seen others do so? What happened?

What do you think God is saying to you through your study of Rom 10:1-4?

PRAYER

Talk to God about what you have read, any questions or concerns you might have, and what you think he might be saying to you today. You can write your prayer here if you wish.

DAY 3 ◆ Romans 10:5-13

READING: **ROMANS 10:5-13**
Begin with prayer, asking God to give you insight, understanding, and an open heart to listen to and follow his word.

STUDY
Why does being right with God through the law require perfect obedience (10:5)? Why then did God give Israel the law, command them to keep it, and promise them long life and prosperity through obeying it?

Romans 10:9 is often quoted as a summary of the Good News. What does it mean to "confess with your mouth that Jesus is Lord"? Why is it a necessary part of salvation?

Why does salvation require you to "believe in your heart that God raised him from the dead"? Why is belief in Jesus' resurrection involved in salvation?

FURTHER STUDY (Optional)
Read Deut 30. What was God saying to Israel through Deut 30:12-14 in the original context?

How does this message relate to the point Paul is making in 10:6-8?

REFLECTION
Does your way of relating to God more resemble an attempt to go up to heaven yourself? Or does it resemble confessing and trusting?

What do you think God is saying to you through your study of Rom 10:5-13?

PRAYER

Talk to God about what you have read, any questions or concerns you might have, and what you think he might be saying to you today. You can write your prayer here if you wish.

DAY 4 ◆ Romans 10:14-17

READING: **ROMANS 10:14-17**

Begin with prayer, asking God to give you insight, understanding, and an open heart to listen to and follow his word.

STUDY

The questions in 10:14-15 are rhetorical—they can be turned into statements. Summarize in one sentence what Paul is saying with this series of questions.

Read the study note on 10:14. Who do you think are the "they" to whom Paul is referring in the questions in 10:14-15?

In 10:15b, Paul quotes Isa 52:7. In light of the questions in 10:14-15a, why *do* the Scriptures say that the feet of messengers who bring good news are beautiful?

FURTHER STUDY (Optional)

What point is Paul making in 10:16 through this quotation of Isa 53:1?

The word translated "faith" (Greek *pistis*) in 10:17 and elsewhere is defined in the *NLT Study Bible* word study dictionary as "confidence that something is real, with a strong implication that action will ensue from this belief. While faith can be rather mundane (e.g., believing a report, 1 Cor 11:18), in the NT it almost always refers to faith in God or Christ. Such faith entails active belief, entrusting oneself completely to God." Also read John 8:30; 12:11; Acts 5:14; 18:8; Rom 1:17; 3:22, 25; 5:1; 14:1; Gal 2:20; Eph 2:8; Phil 1:27; 1 Thes 1:3; 1 Tim 4:6; Heb 6:1; 11:1; Jas 2:14, 20; 1 Jn 3:23.

Why do you think faith requires "hearing the Good News about Christ"?

Faith can be seen as a continuum and a process: Hearing—Welcoming—Believing—Telling—Going. Where would you place yourself on this continuum, and why?

What do you think God is saying to you through your study of Rom 10:14-17?

PRAYER

Talk to God about what you have read, any questions or concerns you might have, and what you think he might be saying to you today. You can write your prayer here if you wish.

DAY 5 ◆ Romans 10:18-21

READING: **ROMANS 10:18-21**

Begin with prayer, asking God to give you insight, understanding, and an open heart to listen to and follow his word.

STUDY

How does the quotation in 10:19 from Deut 32:21 support the point that "the people of Israel really [did] understand"?

What is the connection between the quotation from Isa 65:1-2 and the point Paul is making in 10:19-20?

According to Paul's argument here, why have only few of the Jewish people believed the Good News about Jesus the Messiah?

FURTHER STUDY (Optional)
Reread Rom 9:24-29. How is 10:18-21 saying something similar? How is it saying something different?

REFLECTION
Has jealousy or pride ever kept you from listening to a message that you needed to hear? How could you respond differently?

What do you think God is saying to you through your study of Rom 10:18-21?

PRAYER
Talk to God about what you have read, any questions or concerns you might have, and what you think he might be saying to you today. You can write your prayer here if you wish.

GROUP SESSION

READING: **ROMANS 9:30–10:21**
Read Rom 9:30–10:21 together as a group.

DISCUSSION
You can use the following questions to guide what you share in the discussion. Give each person at least one opportunity to share with the others.

What did you learn from Rom 9:30–10:21? What was one thing that stood out to you as you studied this passage? How did Rom 9:30–10:21 surprise you? Do you have questions about this passage or the study materials that haven't been answered? What does God seem to be saying to you through what you have studied?

TOPICS FOR DISCUSSION

You can choose from among these topics to generate a discussion among the members of your group, or you can write your thoughts about one or more of these topics if you're studying solo.

1. Why did the Jewish people stumble over Christ? How have people that you know stumbled over Christ in a similar way? How can you help them?

2. How would you describe your relationship with God? Do you relate to God on the basis of confession and trust, actions and performance, or some other basis? How do you see your faith in God developing over time?

3. Is God calling you to take his Good News message to others? If so, how and to whom?

GROUP REFLECTION

What is God saying to us as a group through Rom 9:30–10:21?

ACTION

What are we going to do, individually or as a group, in response to what God is saying to us?

PRAYER

How should we pray for each other in response to God's message to us in this passage?

Take turns talking to God about this passage and about what he is saying.

NEXT: **ROMANS 11:1-36 (Israel's Present and Future)**

Israel's Present and Future

ROMANS
11:1-36

OUTLINE

DAY **1** ◆ Romans 11:1-10

READING: **ROMANS 11:1-10**
Begin with prayer, asking God to give you insight, understanding, and an open heart to listen to and follow his word.

STUDY
In 11:1-2, how does Paul support his argument that God has not rejected the nation of Israel?

Did the people of Israel do anything to earn their status as God's people? What does this suggest regarding how they might *keep* their status as God's people?

In 11:2-4, what is Paul's point in citing the example of Elijah's complaint and God's response?

In light of 11:5-10, which people from the nation of Israel are accepted by God? What about the rest?

FURTHER STUDY (Optional)
Read Isa 29:1-10. To whom was Isaiah speaking? What was he saying?

About whom was David speaking in Ps 69:22-23? Why did he pronounce this curse?

How does Paul apply these passages in Rom 11:8-10?

REFLECTION
What does Rom 11:1-10 teach you about God?

What do you think God is saying to you through your study of Rom 11:1-10?

PRAYER

Talk to God about what you have read, any questions or concerns you might have, and what you think he might be saying to you today. You can write your prayer here if you wish.

DAY 2 ◆ Romans 11:11-36

READING: **ROMANS 11:11-36; "JEWS AND GENTILES"**

Read Rom 11:11-36, then read the article, "Jews and Gentiles," p. 1913.
Begin with prayer, asking God to give you insight, understanding, and an open heart to listen to and follow his word.

STUDY

How does Rom 11:11-36 address the theme of Romans, that "God has incorporated Gentiles into the people of God while remaining faithful to his promises to Israel"?

Summarize the stages of God's plan to save all nations. When in this plan are we now living? How do you know?

FURTHER STUDY (Optional)

Read the following passages listed in the margin next to the article on p. 1913. What does each of these passages say in relation to some aspect of God's plan?

Deut 32:19-21 _____

Isa 9:1-3 _____

Matt 4:15-16 _____

Matt 8:10-12 _____

Luke 21:20-24 _____

Acts 13:42-49; 28:23-28 _____

REFLECTION
How is your life involved in God's plan to save all nations?

What do you think God is saying to you through your study of Rom 11:11-36?

PRAYER
Talk to God about what you have read, any questions or concerns you might have, and what you think he might be saying to you today. You can write your prayer here if you wish.

DAY 3 ◆ Romans 11:11-15

READING: **ROMANS 11:11-15**
Begin with prayer, asking God to give you insight, understanding, and an open heart to listen to and follow his word.

STUDY
In what sense is the offer of salvation to the Gentiles the *result* of Israel's disobedience? In what sense is it the *purpose* of Israel's disobedience?

Why would God's offer of salvation to Gentiles make the people of Israel jealous (11:11, 14)? What would such an offer imply about Israel's own relationship with God?

Why do you think Paul foresees a greater blessing when the people of Israel finally accept God's offer of salvation through Jesus Christ (11:12, 15)?

FURTHER STUDY (Optional)
Review your word study of the word translated "offered" (Greek *katallagē*) in 11:15, which you studied in 5:6-11 (p. A41). In light of this word study, what is the significance of Paul's saying that "God offered salvation"?

REFLECTION

What does it tell you about God that he has acted in history in order to accomplish certain purposes in his relationships with both Jewish and Gentile people?

What do you think God is saying to you through your study of Rom 11:11-15?

PRAYER

Talk to God about what you have read, any questions or concerns you might have, and what you think he might be saying to you today. You can write your prayer here if you wish.

DAY 4 ◆ Romans 11:16-24

READING: **ROMANS 11:16-24**

Begin with prayer, asking God to give you insight, understanding, and an open heart to listen to and follow his word.

STUDY

In what sense have some of the "branches from Abraham's tree" been broken off? How have "Gentiles" been grafted in?

According to the study note on 11:18, in what way were the Gentile believers in Rome looking down on the Jewish believers?

How does what Paul says in 11:19-24 correct the Gentile believers' attitude toward the Jews?

FURTHER STUDY (Optional)

Read Gen 12:1-7; 15:1-20; 17:1-8. What is the "blessing God has promised Abraham and his children" (11:17) that Gentile believers now share with Jewish believers? How do we all receive this blessing?

REFLECTION

What attitude does this passage suggest that we have toward the Jewish people and the Old Testament faith? Do you and your community have this kind of attitude? If so, how is it expressed? If not, what could you do to change it?

What do you think God is saying to you through your study of Rom 11:16-24?

PRAYER

Talk to God about what you have read, any questions or concerns you might have, and what you think he might be saying to you today. You can write your prayer here if you wish.

DAY **5** ◆ Romans 11:25-36

READING: **ROMANS 11:25-36**

Begin with prayer, asking God to give you insight, understanding, and an open heart to listen to and follow his word.

STUDY

Again Paul states (11:25-26) that the people of Israel will, in the future, turn to Christ (see 11:12, 15). How will the people of Israel's hearts be softened?

Read 11:29-30. In what sense are the people of Israel who reject Jesus still God's chosen people? In what sense are they not?

Rom 11:31-32 suggests that God has a purpose in the people of Israel's rebellion against Christ. What is that purpose?

FURTHER STUDY (Optional)

What does Paul mean in 11:26 by the phrase "all Israel"?

Read Isa 59:1-21. What is the message of Isa 59? What is Isa 59:20-21 saying in its original context? What is Paul saying in Rom 11:26-27 by quoting it?

REFLECTION

The doxology in 11:33-36 praises God's wisdom and knowledge and describes his decisions and ways as impossible to understand. Do you find it difficult to understand what Paul has been describing about God's relationship with the Jewish people? What is most difficult about it? What does it imply about God's character and nature?

What do you think God is saying to you through your study of Rom 11:25-36?

PRAYER

Talk to God about what you have read, any questions or concerns you might have, and what you think he might be saying to you today. You can write your prayer here if you wish.

GROUP SESSION

READING: **ROMANS 11:1-36**

Read Rom 11:1-36 together as a group.

DISCUSSION

You can use the following questions to guide what you share in the discussion. Give each person at least one opportunity to share with the others.

What did you learn from Rom 11:1-36? What was one thing that stood out to you as you studied this passage? How did Rom 11:1-36 surprise you? Do you have questions about this passage or the study materials that haven't been answered? What does God seem to be saying to you through what you have studied?

TOPICS FOR DISCUSSION

You can choose from among these topics to generate a discussion among the members of your group, or you can write your thoughts about one or more of these topics if you're studying solo.

1. What is God's purpose in the people of Israel's rejection of the Good News? What does this imply for how you live and serve Christ? What does it imply for how you treat others not connected with your Christian community?

2. Is Paul saying that a Jewish or Gentile believer in Christ could be cut off from salvation? If so, how does that square with other passages that imply that a Christian is secure in Christ (e.g., John 6:39; 10:27-29; Rom 8:35-39; Phil 1:6; 1 Pet 1:5)? Or if not, then what is Paul saying in this passage?

3. Since God has ensured that all nations come to him on the basis of his mercy, what are the implications of that for how you share the Good News with others?

GROUP REFLECTION

What is God saying to us as a group through Rom 11:1-36?

ACTION

What are we going to do, individually or as a group, in response to what God is saying to us?

PRAYER

How should we pray for each other in response to God's message to us in this passage?

Take turns talking to God about this passage and about what he is saying.

NEXT: ROMANS 12:1–13:14 (The Transformed Life)

The Transformed Life

ROMANS
12:1–13:14

OUTLINE

DAY **1** ◆ Romans 12:1-2

READING: ROMANS 12:1-2

Begin with prayer, asking God to give you insight, understanding, and an open heart to listen to and follow his word.

STUDY

In 12:1, Paul cites "all [God] has done for you" as the reason for giving God your body. Summarize your understanding of what God has done for you, based on your study of Rom 1–11.

What does it mean to give your body to God? What does making it a "living and holy sacrifice" involve?

What are "the behavior and customs of this world" (12:2) that you should not copy?

What is the key to knowing God's will for your life?

FURTHER STUDY (Optional)

The Greek word for "transform" (Greek *metamorphoō*) means "to change fundamentally and completely from one state to another. It can refer to a physical transformation or to an inward change of character or mind-set" (*NLT Study Bible* word study dictionary). Also read Matt 17:2 and 2 Cor 3:18 for other instances of this word. What does Paul mean in Rom 12:2 when he says that you should "let God transform you into a new person by changing the way you think"?

REFLECTION

In what specific ways can you give your body more fully to God this week? In what ways can you let him transform you?

What do you think God is saying to you through your study of Rom 12:1-2?

PRAYER

Talk to God about what you have read, any questions or concerns you might have, and what you think he might be saying to you today. You can write your prayer here if you wish.

DAY 2 ◆ Romans 12:3-8

READING: **ROMANS 12:3-8**

Begin with prayer, asking God to give you insight, understanding, and an open heart to listen to and follow his word.

STUDY

What is the "privilege and authority God has given" Paul (12:3; see also 1:5)? Why do you think Paul appeals to that here?

Read the study note on 12:1–15:13. What seems to be behind Paul's exhortation in 12:3 not to be vain or self-important?

Romans 12:4-8 says that every part of the body "has a special function" and "different gifts for doing certain things well." What does that imply about how we view others and treat them?

FURTHER STUDY (Optional)

Read 1 Cor 12:4-11, which also lists spiritual gifts. Why does God give us spiritual gifts?

Which of the "different gifts" in Rom 12:6-8 and 1 Cor 12:4-11 seem to match the way God has made you? In what specific ways can you exercise your gifts in a manner that pleases God?

What do you think God is saying to you through your study of Rom 12:3-8?

PRAYER

Talk to God about what you have read, any questions or concerns you might have, and what you think he might be saying to you today. You can write your prayer here if you wish.

DAY 3 ◆ Romans 12:9-21

READING: **ROMANS 12:9-21**

Begin with prayer, asking God to give you insight, understanding, and an open heart to listen to and follow his word.

STUDY

In 12:9, what is the difference between pretending to love others and really loving them?

List the commands in 12:9-21 and summarize how each one exhibits love toward both God and others.

FURTHER STUDY (Optional)

Read 12:17-21. Why should we not take revenge? How should we respond to other people's evil words or actions toward us?

REFLECTION
REFLECTION
What is one thing that you can do differently that will show love toward those around you?

What do you think God is saying to you through your study of Rom 12:9-21?

PRAYER
Talk to God about what you have read, any questions or concerns you might have, and what you think he might be saying to you today. You can write your prayer here if you wish.

DAY 4 ◆ Romans 13:1-7

READING: **ROMANS 13:1-7**
Begin with prayer, asking God to give you insight, understanding, and an open heart to listen to and follow his word.

STUDY
Read the study note on 13:1-2. Why is it generally wrong to disobey the government? Are there situations in which we should not obey what the government says?

If, as the study note on 13:3 says, Paul is only talking about "governing authorities who live according to their calling," what changes in a situation where the governing authorities are doing evil? Or is there no difference?

In what ways do governing authorities serve God (13:4, 6)?

FURTHER STUDY (Optional)
As the study note on 13:1-2 says, "God is actively involved in raising up and casting down human governments." Read the passages listed in that note (1 Sam 2:6-10; 12:8; Prov 8:15-16; Isa 41:2-4; 45:1-7; Jer 21:7, 10; 27:5-6; Dan 2:21, 37-38; 4:17). What do these passages seem to be saying about God's relationship with human governments? What role do God's holy people play in this dynamic?

What is your attitude toward government officials (politicians, bureaucrats, the police, the IRS, etc.)? What attitude does Paul's teaching promote?

What do you think God is saying to you through your study of Rom 13:1-7?

PRAYER

Talk to God about what you have read, any questions or concerns you might have, and what you think he might be saying to you today. You can write your prayer here if you wish.

DAY 5 ◆ Romans 13:8-14

READING: ROMANS 13:8-14

Begin with prayer, asking God to give you insight, understanding, and an open heart to listen to and follow his word.

STUDY

How does the command of 13:8 connect to Paul's instruction in 13:6-7?

Read the study note on 13:8-10. How does loving others fulfill the law?

Why does the shortness of time (13:11) make the command to love urgent?

In 13:12-14, how does moral purity relate to the urgent need to show love toward others? Why is moral impurity inconsistent with Paul's command to "clothe yourself with the presence of the Lord Jesus Christ"?

FURTHER STUDY (Optional)

Read 13:8-10 and Matt 22:34-40. Summarize the parallels between Jesus' teaching and Paul's teaching in these two passages.

REFLECTION

What specific changes do Paul's commands here (to love others, live with purity, and clothe yourself with Jesus Christ) suggest in your life?

What do you think God is saying to you through your study of Rom 13:8-14?

PRAYER

Talk to God about what you have read, any questions or concerns you might have, and what you think he might be saying to you today. You can write your prayer here if you wish.

GROUP SESSION

READING: **ROMANS 12:1–13:14**

Read Rom 12:1–13:14 together as a group.

DISCUSSION

You can use the following questions to guide what you share in the discussion. Give each person at least one opportunity to share with the others.

What did you learn from Rom 12:1–13:14? What was one thing that stood out to you as you studied this passage? How did Rom 12:1–13:14 surprise you? Do you have questions about this passage or the study materials that haven't been answered? What does God seem to be saying to you through what you have studied?

TOPICS FOR DISCUSSION

You can choose from among these topics to generate a discussion among the members of your group, or you can write your thoughts about one or more of these topics if you're studying solo.

1. How can you give your body to God, let him transform your mind, and live in the light of Christ's presence more fully?

2. Paul repeatedly urges Christians to love others fully (12:9-21; 13:8-10). What specific things is God prompting you to do in response to these instructions?

3. Every part of the Christian community has a special function, just like every part of the human body. What function(s) has God made you to do? How can you show greater honor to other members of the community who have different gifts from yours?

GROUP REFLECTION

What is God saying to us as a group through Rom 12:1–13:14?

ACTION

What are we going to do, individually or as a group, in response to what God is saying to us?

PRAYER

How should we pray for each other in response to God's message to us in this passage?

Take turns talking to God about this passage and about what he is saying.

NEXT: **ROMANS 14:1–15:13 (Scruples and Freedoms)**

WEEK

ELEVEN

*Scruples
and
Freedoms*

ROMANS
14:1–15:13

OUTLINE

DAY **1** ◆ Romans 14:1–15:13

READING: **ROMANS 14:1–15:13; "TOLERANCE AND ITS LIMITS"**
Read through Rom 14:1–15:13, then read the article, "Tolerance and Its Limits," p. 1919.
Also read the study note on 14:1–15:7.
Begin with prayer, asking God to give you insight, understanding, and an open heart to listen to and follow his word.

STUDY
What issue in the church in Rome was this passage written to address?

What kinds of issues does Paul urge the Roman Christians to exercise tolerance about?

Based on Paul's teachings elsewhere, what kinds of issues should *not* receive toleration or accommodation?

REFLECTION
Can you think of specific issues that *should* be addressed with toleration and accommodation in the church and are not? Are there issues that *should not* be addressed with toleration and accommodation and yet are? What changes could be made to handle these issues rightly?

What do you think God is saying to you through your study of Rom 14:1–15:13?

PRAYER
Talk to God about what you have read, any questions or concerns you might have, and what you think he might be saying to you today. You can write your prayer here if you wish.

DAY 2 ◆ Romans 14:1-12

READING: **ROMANS 14:1-12**

Begin with prayer, asking God to give you insight, understanding, and an open heart to listen to and follow his word.

STUDY

What does Paul mean by describing certain believers as "weak in faith" (14:1)?

Why would some of the believers in Rome "eat only vegetables" (14:2)?

Why would believers "who feel free to eat anything" disdain those who didn't (14:3-4)? Why would those who didn't eat everything "condemn" those who did?

Those who are believers belong to the Lord and live for him (14:7-9). What are the implications for our relationships with different groups of Christians?

FURTHER STUDY (Optional)

What are the implications for our attitude toward other believers, that we will each stand before God and give account for our own lives (14:10-12)?

Read the study note on 14:11; then read Isa 45:18-25. What is the point of Isa 45:23 in its original context? What is the point Paul is making by quoting it here?

REFLECTION

What issue in your community is similar to the food issue in Rome, with people on both sides of the "scruples" vs. "freedom" divide? How do the two groups treat each other? How *should* they treat each other?

What do you think God is saying to you through your study of Rom 14:1-12?

PRAYER

Talk to God about what you have read, any questions or concerns you might have, and what you think he might be saying to you today. You can write your prayer here if you wish.

DAY 3 ◆ Romans 14:13-23

READING: **ROMANS 14:13-23**

Begin with prayer, asking God to give you insight, understanding, and an open heart to listen to and follow his word.

STUDY

What role does conscience have in defining sin (see 14:14, 23)? Why do you think it has that role? In other words, why do you think there is a subjective element in determining what is and isn't sin?

According to the study note on 14:15, how could freedom regarding food "ruin someone for whom Christ died"? Can you think of an analogous situation in your own cultural context?

Some people have used 14:15-23 to argue that a Christian should never do something that another Christian would have a scruple against. Is that what Paul is saying? If not, how is what Paul is saying different from that?

REFLECTION

What specific issues in your life or relationships with others do the instructions of this passage address?

What do you think God is saying to you through your study of Rom 14:13-23?

Talk to God about what you have read, any questions or concerns you might have, and what you think he might be saying to you today. You can write your prayer here if you wish.

DAY 4 ◆ Romans 15:1-6

READING: **ROMANS 15:1-6**
Begin with prayer, asking God to give you insight, understanding, and an open heart to listen to and follow his word.

STUDY
How do you think Paul envisions that the "stronger" believers would "help others do what is right and build them up in the Lord" (15:1-2)?

What is Paul's point in saying, "even Christ didn't live to please himself" (15:3)?

How does the quotation of Ps 69:9 support the point that Paul is making?

FURTHER STUDY (Optional)
Read the study note on 15:5-6. Also read Phil 2:2-5. What is a "mindset of harmony"? How do we cultivate it?

REFLECTION
How does living in harmony with other believers with whom we don't agree make us more like our Lord Jesus Christ?

What do you think God is saying to you through your study of Rom 15:1-6?

PRAYER

Talk to God about what you have read, any questions or concerns you might have, and what you think he might be saying to you today. You can write your prayer here if you wish.

DAY 5 ◆ Romans 15:7-13

READING: **ROMANS 15:7-13**

Begin with prayer, asking God to give you insight, understanding, and an open heart to listen to and follow his word.

STUDY

Reread Rom 5:8-11. How has Christ "accepted you" (15:7)? What would it look like to extend the same acceptance to others?

Read the passages cited in the NLT margin for 15:8 (Matt 15:24; Acts 3:25-26; 2 Cor 1:20). What do these passages suggest about how "Christ came as a servant to the Jews to show that God is true to the promises he made"?

How do hope, joy, and peace (15:13) flow out of what Paul has been saying in 15:7-12?

FURTHER STUDY (Optional)

As the study note on 15:9-12 states, the quotations in this passage support Gentiles being full members of God's family. How does each of these quotations do that?

15:9 // Ps 18:49 _____

15:10 // Deut 32:43 _____

15:11 // Ps 117:1 _____

15:12 // Isa 11:10 _____

REFLECTION
What is the status of your confidence in God's acceptance? How would you describe your sense of standing before God? To what extent do you have peace about it?

What do you think God is saying to you through your study of Rom 15:7-13?

PRAYER
Talk to God about what you have read, any questions or concerns you might have, and what you think he might be saying to you today. You can write your prayer here if you wish.

GROUP SESSION

READING: **ROMANS 14:1–15:13**
Read Rom 14:1–15:13 together as a group.

DISCUSSION
You can use the following questions to guide what you share in the discussion. Give each person at least one opportunity to share with the others.

What did you learn from Rom 14:1–15:13? What was one thing that stood out to you as you studied this passage? How did Rom 14:1–15:13 surprise you? Do you have questions about this passage or the study materials that haven't been answered? What does God seem to be saying to you through what you have studied?

TOPICS FOR DISCUSSION

You can choose from among these topics to generate a discussion among the members of your group, or you can write your thoughts about one or more of these topics if you're studying solo.

1. Every Christian community faces conflict between those who have scruples and those who feel freedom. What are the issues in your own life or in your community? How have people hurt each other over these issues?

2. How does Paul instruct us in 14:1–15:13 to handle differences regarding scruples and freedoms?

3. How does living in harmony with others reflect Jesus Christ himself? In what specific ways can you extend acceptance to others who are different from you, reflecting the acceptance that Jesus Christ has extended to you?

GROUP REFLECTION

What is God saying to us as a group through Rom 14:1–15:13?

ACTION

What are we going to do, individually or as a group, in response to what God is saying to us?

PRAYER

How should we pray for each other in response to God's message to us in this passage?

Take turns talking to God about this passage and about what he is saying.

NEXT: **ROMANS 15:14–16:27 (Paul's Plans, Greetings, and Doxology)**

Paul's Plans, Greetings, and Doxology

ROMANS
15:14–16:27

OUTLINE

DAY **1** ✦ Romans 15:14-22

READING: **ROMANS 15:14-22**

Begin with prayer, asking God to give you insight, understanding, and an open heart to listen to and follow his word.

STUDY

In 15:14-16, how does Paul describe his purpose in writing the letter to the Romans? What did the Roman Christians need from Paul that they did not have already?

In what sense had Paul "fully presented the Good News of Christ" in the areas where he had served (15:19)?

How was Paul's mission—to preach where Christ was unknown—a fulfillment of the plan of Scripture (15:20-21)?

FURTHER STUDY (Optional)

Read Isa 52:13–53:12, a passage that Christians understand as predicting Christ's work. What is Isa 52:15 saying about Christ? How does Paul's work fulfill this vision?

REFLECTION

Paul had a strong, clear sense of his purpose in serving Christ. Do you? If so, what is it? If not, how can you seek it?

What do you think God is saying to you through your study of Rom 15:14-22?

PRAYER

Talk to God about what you have read, any questions or concerns you might have, and what you think he might be saying to you today. You can write your prayer here if you wish.

DAY 2 ◆ Romans 15:23-33

READING: **ROMANS 15:23-33**
    Begin with prayer, asking God to give you insight, understanding, and an open heart to listen to and follow his word.

STUDY
    In light of 15:20-21, why did Paul want to go to Spain (15:24)?

    Read 15:25-28 and the study note. What purposes did Paul have for delivering a financial gift from the Gentile churches to the Jewish Christians in Jerusalem?

    What prayers did Paul want the Roman Christians to pray for him, and for what purposes (15:30-32)?

FURTHER STUDY (Optional)
    Read Acts 21–23, describing Paul's arrival in Jerusalem after writing the letter to the Romans. What does this passage show you about the need for the prayers that he requested in Rom 15:30-32? In what manner did God answer Paul's prayer for "rescue from those in Judea who refuse to obey God"?

    Read Acts 27–28, which describes Paul's journey from Jerusalem to Rome. How did God "richly bless" Paul's "time together" with the Roman Christians (Rom 15:29) and make them "an encouragement to each other" (15:32)?

REFLECTION
    Have you ever had a goal that you prayed for God's help with, or even asked others to pray with you about, and then God answered your prayer in unexpected ways? If so, did that experience strengthen your faith, or shake it?

    What do you think God is saying to you through your study of Rom 15:23-33?

Talk to God about what you have read, any questions or concerns you might have, and what you think he might be saying to you today. You can write your prayer here if you wish.

DAY 3 ◆ Romans 16:1-16

READING: ROMANS 16:1-16

Begin with prayer, asking God to give you insight, understanding, and an open heart to listen to and follow his word.

STUDY

Read the study note on 16:1-16. Paul personally knew and greeted 27 Christians who were in Rome at the time. What does that tell you about Paul and his ministry?

In what ways had Phoebe demonstrated that she was truly a "deacon" (servant) of the Christian community (16:1-2)?

What does it mean that Andronicus and Junia were "highly respected among the apostles" (16:7)? What group does the word "apostles" refer to in this context?

What did Paul have in mind when instructing Christians to "greet each other in Christian love" (16:16)? How could we fulfill this instruction in our day?

FURTHER STUDY (Optional)

Read 16:1 and the study note. The word "deacon" (Greek *diakonos*) refers to a person who serves, assists, and helps others. In addition to referring to a recognized servant of God and his people, it can also refer to a leadership office in the Christian community. Also read Matt 20:26; Acts 6:1-6; Phil 1:1; Col 1:7, 23; 4:7; 1 Tim 3:8-12; 4:6. In what sense do you think Phoebe was a "deacon in the church in Cenchrea"? Did she hold the office of "deacon," or was she more of a recognized "servant" but not an officer? Why do you think as you do?

REFLECTION

If Paul were sending greetings to your home church and he knew you personally, what would he say about you? What would you *want* him to say about you? If the two answers are different, how can you bring the first into line with the second?

What do you think God is saying to you through your study of Rom 16:1-16?

PRAYER
Talk to God about what you have read, any questions or concerns you might have, and what you think he might be saying to you today. You can write your prayer here if you wish.

DAY 4 ◆ Romans 16:17-20

READING: ROMANS 16:17-20
Begin with prayer, asking God to give you insight, understanding, and an open heart to listen to and follow his word.

STUDY
Read 16:17-18 and the study note on 16:17. How did (and do) some people try to cause divisions in the Christian community? See also 1 Cor 1:10-13; 11:17-22; Gal 5:19-21; 1 Tim 6:3-5; Jude 1:17-19.

Why do you think Paul instructed Christians to "stay away from" these divisive people?

Read the study note on 16:20. In light of 16:17-19, what is Paul referring to when he foresees God crushing Satan under the Christians' feet? What would this have meant in the context of the Roman Christian community?

FURTHER STUDY (Optional)
The word "Satan" (Greek *satanas*) in 16:20 refers, according to the *NLT Study Bible* word study dictionary, "to an adversary in general, but in the NT it functions as a title for the devil, the great adversary of God and his people." For more examples of this word, also read Matt 4:10; 16:23; Luke 10:18; John 13:27; Acts 5:3; 2 Cor 11:14-15; 12:7; 1 Thes 2:18; Rev 2:24; 20:2, 7.

What is the work of Satan in the world? How do Christians overcome him?

REFLECTION

Are there divisive people or false teachers in your Christian community? If not, what other challenges that might be from Satan are you or your community facing? How can you individually and your community respond effectively?

What do you think God is saying to you through your study of Rom 16:17-20?

PRAYER

Talk to God about what you have read, any questions or concerns you might have, and what you think he might be saying to you today. You can write your prayer here if you wish.

DAY 5 ◆ Romans 16:21-27

READING: **ROMANS 16:21-27**

Begin with prayer, asking God to give you insight, understanding, and an open heart to listen to and follow his word.

STUDY

Each of the people that Paul mentions in 16:21-23 was a friend and co-worker of Paul. Read the study notes on 16:21-23, read the following passages, and summarize what we learn about these people and their relationship with Paul: Acts 13:1-3; 16:1-3; 17:5; 20:4-5; 1 Cor 4:17; 16:10-11; Phil 2:19-23; 1 Thes 3:2-6.

The note on 16:25-27 says that this doxology makes an "appropriate conclusion to Paul's letter and its argument, reprising many of the themes." Read 1:1-15 again, then read 16:25-27 and summarize the themes that this doxology reprises.

What is God's "plan for you Gentiles" (16:25-26)?

FURTHER STUDY (Optional)

The word translated "revealed" (Greek *apokalupsis*) in 16:25, according to the *NLT Study Bible* word study dictionary, means "a state or action of making something known, usually with the implication that it had been hidden or unknown. It is also the Greek title of the book of Revelation." Also read Luke 2:32; 1 Cor 1:7; 14:6, 26; 2 Cor 12:1, 7; Gal 1:12; Eph 1:17; 3:3; 1 Pet 1:13; 4:13; Rev 1:1.

What does it mean that the Good News about Jesus Christ has "revealed" God's plan?

REFLECTION
In what ways does the Good News and God's plan in your life bring glory to God?

What do you think God is saying to you through your study of Rom 16:21-27?

PRAYER
Talk to God about what you have read, any questions or concerns you might have, and what you think he might be saying to you today. You can write your prayer here if you wish.

GROUP SESSION

READING: **ROMANS 15:14–16:27**
Read Rom 15:14–16:27 together as a group.

DISCUSSION
You can use the following questions to guide what you share in the discussion. Give each person at least one opportunity to share with the others.

What did you learn from Rom 15:14–16:27? What was one thing that stood out to you as you studied this passage? How did Rom 15:14–16:27 surprise you? Do you have questions about this passage or the study materials that haven't been answered? What does God seem to be saying to you through what you have studied?

TOPICS FOR DISCUSSION

You can choose from among these topics to generate a discussion among the members of your group, or you can write your thoughts about one or more of these topics if you're studying solo.

1. How has God "revealed his plan for you" (16:25) through your study of the letter to the Romans?

2. Paul had a strong, clear sense of his purpose in serving Christ. Do you? If so, what is it? If not, how can you seek it? How can you present yourself as an "acceptable offering to God" (15:16)?

3. How can we embody what we have learned in Romans to those around us? How can we represent Jesus and his plan in a faithful, loving way?

GROUP REFLECTION

What is God saying to us as a group through Rom 15:14–16:27?

ACTION

What are we going to do, individually or as a group, in response to what God is saying to us?

PRAYER

How should we pray for each other in response to God's message to us in this passage?

Take turns talking to God about this passage and about what he is saying.

LETTER TO THE ROMANS

PAUL'S LETTER TO THE

ROMANS

Romans has been called the greatest theological document
ever written. In this letter, the apostle Paul explains the
Good News—the climactic revelation of God to the world
through his Son, the Lord Jesus Christ. Paul reflects on the
human condition, on the meaning of our lives on earth, and
on our hope for the world to come. He constantly moves us
back to the fundamentals of God's truth revealed in Christ,
and he teaches us to deal with the problems, failures, and
disputes that characterize life in this world.

SETTING

We do not know who first brought the Good News to Rome. Perhaps
Jews from Rome who were converted when God first poured out his
Spirit on the day of Pentecost (see Acts 2:10) took the message back to
their home city. Several "house churches" quickly grew up, made up
primarily of converts from Judaism.

In AD 49, the Emperor Claudius expelled all Jews from Rome—including Jewish Christians (see Acts 18:2). Although Paul had never visited
Rome (1:13), in his travels he met some of these Roman Christians, such
as Priscilla and Aquila (16:3-4; cp. Acts 18:2).

Claudius's decree eventually lapsed, so by the time Paul wrote his
letter to the Romans, many Jewish Christians had returned to Rome.
However, in their absence the Gentile Christians had taken the lead in
the Christian community in Rome. Therefore, when Paul wrote to the
Roman Christians (probably about AD 57), the Roman Christian community was divided into two major factions. The Gentile Christians now
comprised the majority group, and they were naturally less concerned
about continuity with the OT or with the demands of the law of Moses
than their Jewish brothers and sisters. They even looked down on the
Jewish Christians (see 11:25). The minority Jewish Christians, for their
part, reacted to the Gentile-Christian ma-
jority by insisting on adherence to certain
aspects of the law of Moses. Paul wrote
this letter to the Roman Christians to address this theological and social division, a
schism that had at its heart the question of
continuity and discontinuity between Jewish and Christian faith.

◀ The Setting of Romans, about AD 57. Paul probably
wrote Romans toward the end of his third missionary
journey (Acts 18:23–19:41), perhaps from CORINTH. Paul
had the opportunity to visit the Romans, as he hoped
(1:10-15)—his third missionary journey ended in JERU-
SALEM, where he was imprisoned and eventually sent to
ROME, where he arrived in AD 60 (Acts 28:11-15).

SUMMARY

In the introduction of the letter (1:1-17), Paul identifies himself and his readers (1:1-7), expresses thanks for the Roman Christians (1:8-15), and introduces the theme of the letter: the "Good News about Christ" (1:16-17).

Before elaborating on this Good News, Paul sets out the dark backdrop of universal human sinfulness that makes the Good News necessary. Both Gentiles (1:18-32) and Jews (2:1–3:8) have turned away from God's revelation of himself. All are "under the power of sin" and cannot be made right with God by anything they do (3:9-20).

Into this hopeless situation comes the Good News, which reveals a new "way to be made right" with God. God provided this new way by sending Jesus as a sacrifice for sin, and all human beings can gain the benefits of that sacrifice by faith (3:21-26). Paul highlights the centrality of faith and its nature in 3:27–4:25. He shows that faith excludes boasting and that it enables both Jews and Gentiles to have equal access to God's grace in Christ (3:27-31). He develops these same points through reference to Abraham (4:1-25).

In chs 5–8, Paul discusses the assurance or security of salvation. The assurance that believers will share God's glory (5:1-11) is based on the way in which Jesus Christ more than reversed the terrible effects of Adam's sin (5:12-21). Neither sin (6:1-23) nor the law (7:1-25) can prevent God from accomplishing his purposes for the believer. The Holy Spirit liberates believers from death (8:1-17) and assures them that the sufferings of this life will not keep them from the glory to which God has destined them (8:18-39).

The Good News can only truly be "good news" if the message of Christ stands in continuity with God's promises in the OT. But the unbelief of so many Jews might show that God's promises to Israel are not being fulfilled (9:1-5). So, in chs 9–11, Paul demonstrates that God is being faithful to his promises. God had never promised salvation to all Jews, but only to a remnant (9:6-29). The Jews themselves are responsible for their predicament because they refuse to recognize the fulfillment of God's promises in Christ (9:30–10:21). Furthermore, God is faithfully preserving a remnant of Jewish believers (11:1-10), and God has still more to accomplish for his people Israel (11:11-36).

The Good News rescues people from the penalty of sin, and it also transforms a person's life. In 12:1–15:13, Paul turns his attention to the transforming power of the Good News. In keeping with God's mercies, this transformation demands a whole new way of thinking and living (12:1-2).

OUTLINE

1:1-17
The Letter Opening

1:18–4:25
The Heart of the Gospel: Justification by Faith

5:1–8:39
The Assurance Provided by the Gospel: The Hope of Salvation

9:1–11:36
The Defense of the Gospel: The Problem of Israel

12:1–15:13
The Transforming Power of the Gospel: Christian Conduct

15:14–16:27
The Letter Closing

TIMELINE

Pentecost, AD 30 or 33
The birth of the church in Jerusalem

about AD 31 or 34
Probable founding of the church in Rome

AD 49
Emperor Claudius expels Jews from Rome

AD 53–57
Paul's third missionary journey

about AD 57
▶ **Paul writes Romans from Corinth**

AD 57
Paul travels to Jerusalem and is arrested

AD 57–59
Paul is imprisoned in Caesarea

AD 59–60
Paul's voyage to Rome

AD 60–62
Paul is imprisoned in Rome

AD 62~64
Paul is released, travels freely

July AD 64
Fire destroys Rome

AD 64~65
Persecution of Christians under Nero
Peter is crucified in Rome

about AD 64~65?
Paul is imprisoned and martyred in Rome

The transformed life will be fleshed out in community harmony (12:3-8), manifestations of love (12:9-21; cp. 13:8-10), and submission to the government (13:1-7). The transformed life derives its power from the work God has already done, as well as from the work he has yet to do (13:11-14).

In 14:1–15:13, Paul tackles a specific issue that was a problem in the church at Rome. Christians were criticizing each other over various practices related to the OT law. Paul exhorts them to accept each other and to look to Christ's example of self-giving love as the model to emulate.

The letter format of Romans emerges again at the end, where Paul touches on his ministry and travel plans (15:14-33), greets and commends fellow workers and other Christians (16:1-16), and concludes with further references to fellow workers, a final warning, and a doxology (16:17-27).

DATE, PLACE, AND OCCASION OF WRITING

Paul probably wrote Romans during a three-month stay in Corinth near the end of his third missionary journey (Acts 20:2-3), around AD 57. The reference to Cenchrea in 16:1—a port city next to Corinth—identifies the geography more precisely. By this time, Paul had completed his missionary work in the eastern Mediterranean, and his visit to Jerusalem was imminent.

We can determine the general situation in which Romans was written by reviewing Paul's references to his prior ministry and his future travel plans (15:14-33). Four geographical references provide the framework: (1) Looking back, Paul declared that he had "fully presented the Good News of Christ from Jerusalem all the way to Illyricum" (15:19). Illyricum was a Roman province that occupied the same general area as modern-day Serbia and Croatia. Paul noted that he had planted churches in major cities from Jerusalem, through Asia Minor, and into Macedonia and Greece. This was the territory Paul and his companions covered on the three great missionary journeys recorded in Acts. (2) Paul's intermediate destination was Jerusalem, where he planned to deliver a "gift to the believers" (15:25). This gift was money that Paul had been collecting from the Gentile churches he had founded to assist the church in Jerusalem (15:26; see also 1 Cor 16:1-4; 2 Cor 8–9). (3) After visiting Jerusalem to deliver the collection, Paul planned to go to Rome (15:24). (4) A long stay with the Roman Christians was not Paul's final goal, as the language of 15:24 ("stop off") makes clear. His ultimate goal was Spain, where he could pursue his calling to plant churches in places "where the name of Christ has never been heard" (15:20, 24). This information points to a date near the end of the third missionary journey.

PAUL'S PURPOSE IN WRITING

Romans combines three specific purposes: to summarize Paul's theology, to solicit support for a future mission to Spain, and to bring unity to the church in Rome.

Paul saw himself standing at a critical juncture in his ministry (15:20). He had "fully presented" or fulfilled the Good News by taking it to a broad area of the eastern Mediterranean basin (15:19). He now stood ready to move to the far end of the Mediterranean to preach the

[Romans] is worthy not only that every Christian should know it word for word, by heart, but occupy himself with it every day, as the daily bread of the soul. It can never be read or pondered too much, and the more it is dealt with the more precious it becomes, and the better it tastes.

MARTIN LUTHER
"Preface to the Epistle to the Romans"

Good News in new territory. It is quite natural, then, that Paul took the occasion of his letter to the Romans to summarize his theology as he had hammered it out in the midst of controversy and trial for the previous twenty-five years.

In other words, Romans might be a summary of Paul's theology. Even so, this is not the whole of Paul's purpose in writing—it does not explain why Paul says so little in Romans about key theological ideas (e.g., the person of Christ, the church, the last days). Nor does it explain why Paul would have sent this summary of his theology to the church in Rome.

Another purpose emerges when we turn our attention to Paul's ultimate destination, Spain: Paul wanted to gather support from the Roman Christians for his new mission in a distant land. Paul's "sending church," Antioch, was thousands of miles from Spain. As the apostle sought a new church to partner with him, his attention naturally turned to the church in Rome (15:24). Therefore, it is likely that Paul sent this dense theological treatise to Rome because he wanted to explain who he was and what he believed. Because Paul's message had frequently been misunderstood, he became a controversial figure in the early church. He was undoubtedly aware that some Christians in Rome were suspicious of him and that he therefore must provide a careful and reasoned defense of his position on some of the most debated issues of the faith.

Finally, Paul wrote to a Christian community in Rome that was divided over the degree to which the OT law should continue to guide believers. Paul's long and explicit treatment of this problem (14:1–15:13) reveals that one of his purposes in writing was to heal this rift in the community in Rome.

In Romans, Paul presented the Good News as he had come to understand it. The heart of that Good News is the offer of salvation in Christ for all who believe. Paul explores the problem of human sin, the solution provided in the cross of Christ, and the assurance of glory that a living relationship with Christ provides. The message of the cross of Christ stands both in continuity with the OT (because its promises are truly fulfilled in Christ) and in discontinuity with it (as God in Christ inaugurates a new covenant that transcends the OT law).

INTERPRETATION

Since the time of the Reformation, Romans has been read as a letter about the salvation of the individual. Following the lead of Martin Luther, whose own spiritual pilgrimage was closely tied to the theology of Romans, the Reformers (such as John Calvin and Ulrich Zwingli) saw in this letter the classic biblical expression of the truth that human beings are put right with God by their faith in Christ and not by their own effort. The Reformers viewed Paul as fighting against a legalistic Judaism that insisted that people had to obey the law to be saved. Jewish preoccupation with the law had led many Jews to presume that faithfulness to the law was sufficient for salvation (e.g., 10:1-4).

Many contemporary interpreters insist that this Reformation view of Romans left out important elements in understanding both the letter itself and first-century Judaism. Jews in Paul's day, it is argued, did not believe that they had to obey the law to be saved. They were already saved, through God's choosing them to be his people. Obeying the

The reasons why Romans is such a powerful piece of writing, and why it has been so influential in Christian history, are one and the same. . . . We see Paul the Jew wrestling with the implications of his own and his converts' experience of grace and Paul the Christian wrestling with the implications of his Jewish heritage. We see in Romans Paul operating at the interface between Pharisaic Judaism and Christianity, and the transition from the one to the other in process of being worked out.

JAMES D. G. DUNN
Romans, p. xvi

law was the way they maintained their status as God's people. These interpreters say that Paul was not fighting against legalism but against exclusivism—against the Jewish claim that salvation was confined to Israel and was not to be shared with Gentiles. Accordingly, Paul shows how the Good News relates salvation through faith to the continuity of God's people from the OT to the NT and to the relationship of Jews and Gentiles in his own day.

This new approach to understanding Romans has much to commend it. Christian interpreters have sometimes missed the notes of grace and faith that are part of Jewish teaching. And Romans does have a lot to say about including Gentiles in God's people and the relationship between Jews and Gentiles in the church.

Ultimately, however, neither the Reformation view alone nor the contemporary view alone explains everything in Romans. They need to be combined if we are to appreciate the letter as a whole. At its most foundational level, Romans is about the Good News—and the Good News, first and foremost, is a message about how everyone can have a right relationship with God.

FURTHER READING

ROGER MOHRLANG
Romans in *Cornerstone Biblical Commentary*, vol. 14 (2007)

DOUGLAS J. MOO
The Epistle to the Romans (1996)

JOHN MURRAY
The Epistle to the Romans (1959, 1965)

THOMAS SCHREINER
Romans (1998)

JOHN R. W. STOTT
Romans: God's Good News for the World (1994)

1. THE LETTER OPENING (1:1-17)
Greetings from Paul

1 This letter is from Paul, a ᵃslave of Christ Jesus, chosen by God to be an apostle and sent out to preach his ᵇGood News. ²God promised this Good News long ago through his prophets in the holy Scriptures. ³The Good News is about his Son. In his earthly life he was born into King David's family line, ⁴and he was shown to be the Son of God when he was raised from the dead by the power of the Holy Spirit. He is Jesus Christ our Lord. ⁵Through Christ, God has given us the privilege and authority as apostles to tell Gentiles everywhere what God has done for them, so that they will believe and obey him, bringing glory to his name.

⁶And you are included among those Gentiles who have been ᶜcalled to belong to Jesus Christ. ⁷I am writing to all of you in Rome who are loved by God and are called to be his own holy people.

May God our Father and the Lord Jesus Christ give you grace and peace.

1:1
ᵃ*doulos* (1401)
▸ Rom 6:20
ᵇ*euangelion* (2098)
▸ Rom 1:16
1:2
Titus 1:2
1:3
Matt 1:1; 22:42
1:4
1 Cor 15:1-4, 12-23
1:5
Acts 9:15; 26:15-18
1:6
ᶜ*klētos* (2822)
▸ Rom 8:28

. . . .

1:1-17 These verses contain the normal features of NT letter introductions: an identification of the writer (1:1-6) and readers (1:7); a thanksgiving (1:8-15); and the theme of the letter (1:16-17).

1:1 *slave of Christ Jesus:* The word *slave* is used of important OT leaders of God's people, such as Moses (2 Kgs 18:12), Joshua (Josh 24:29), Elijah (2 Kgs 10:10), and David (2 Sam 7:8). The title underscores Paul's complete subservience to Christ as Lord. • *sent out* (literally *set apart*): Paul may be alluding to being "set apart" by God for his mission before he was born, as the prophet Jeremiah was (Jer 1:5). He may also be referring to God's call at the time of his Damascus Road conversion (Acts 9:15-16; cp. Acts 13:2), to preach the Good News to Jews and especially to Gentiles. • The *Good News*, or "gospel," is a recurrent topic in the opening of the letter (1:1, 9, 15, 16). Paul takes the word from the OT, where the Hebrew equivalent refers to the victory that God wins for his people (Isa 40:9; 41:27; 60:6; 61:1; Nah 1:15; see Joel 2:32).

1:3-4 In the Greek, these verses are in carefully structured parallel form; Paul might be quoting an early Christian creed or hymn about Jesus Christ as God's *Son* in order to establish common ground with the Roman Christians, whom he had never visited.

1:3 *In his earthly life* (literally *As regards the flesh*): Paul often uses "flesh" (Greek *sarx*) to refer to bodily existence in this world (e.g., 4:1; 8:3). • Paul refers to *King David's family line* because God promised that a descendant of David would be the Messiah and would be given an eternal kingdom (2 Sam 7:13-16; see Isa 9:7; Jer 33:15). Jesus was born into David's line (Matt 1:6; Luke 1:27, 32), so he was qualified to fulfill God's promise.

1:4 *and he was shown to be* (or *and was designated*): Although he eternally existed as the Son of God (1:3), Jesus' resurrection demonstrated him to be God's Son, revealing him in all his power and glory. • *by the power of the Holy Spirit:* Or *by the Spirit of holiness;* or *in the new realm of the Spirit.*

1:5 *given us . . . apostles:* Here Paul might have been thinking both of himself and of the other apostles, or he might be using an editorial plural to refer only to himself. • *the privilege* (or *the grace*): Privilege and *authority* could specify two separate things, but one might explain the other, as in the privilege of having apostolic authority. Paul always makes it clear that his distinctive authority is a gift from God (see also 15:15-16). • *so that they will believe and obey him:* This summary of Paul's purpose in preaching to Gentiles brackets the book of Romans, as he repeats the same idea in slightly different language at the end of the letter (16:26). Paul wanted Gentiles to believe in Jesus Christ; he underscored that believing in Jesus Christ as the Lord entails a commitment to obey him. Faith and obedience are not identical, but one does not occur without the other.

1:7 To be *holy* means to be set apart for God. This expression is used throughout the OT to describe Israel, God's chosen *people* (cp. Exod 19:6), whom God called from among all other nations to be his own. By calling the Gentile Christians *his own holy people*, Paul makes it clear that Gentiles are now fully included among God's people.

1:8
1 Thes 1:8
1:9
Phil 1:8-9
1:11
ᵈcharisma (5486)
▸ Rom 12:6
1:14
1 Cor 9:16
1:15
Rom 15:20
1:16
Acts 3:26
1 Cor 1:18, 24
ᵉeuangelion (2098)
▸ Rom 2:16
ˢsōtēria (4991)
▸ Rom 8:24
1:17
*Hab 2:4
Rom 3:21-22
Gal 3:11
Heb 10:38
ᵍdikaiosunē (1343)
▸ Rom 3:21
ʰpistis (4102)
▸ Rom 3:22
1:18
Eph 5:6
Col 3:6
ⁱorgē (3709)
▸ Rom 2:5
1:19
Acts 14:15-17;
17:24-28
1:20
Job 12:7-9
Ps 19:1

Thanksgiving and Occasion: Paul and the Romans

⁸Let me say first that I thank my God through Jesus Christ for all of you, because your faith in him is being talked about all over the world. ⁹God knows how often I pray for you. Day and night I bring you and your needs in prayer to God, whom I serve with all my heart by spreading the Good News about his Son.

¹⁰One of the things I always pray for is the opportunity, God willing, to come at last to see you. ¹¹For I long to visit you so I can bring you some spiritual ᵈgift that will help you grow strong in the Lord. ¹²When we get together, I want to encourage you in your faith, but I also want to be encouraged by yours.

¹³I want you to know, dear brothers and sisters, that I planned many times to visit you, but I was prevented until now. I want to work among you and see spiritual fruit, just as I have seen among other Gentiles. ¹⁴For I have a great sense of obligation to people in both the civilized world and the rest of the world, to the educated and uneducated

alike. ¹⁵So I am eager to come to you in Rome, too, to preach the Good News.

The Theme of the Letter: God's Good News

¹⁶For I am not ashamed of this ᵉGood News about Christ. It is the power of God at work, ᶠsaving everyone who believes—the Jew first and also the Gentile. ¹⁷This Good News tells us how God makes us ᵍright in his sight. This is accomplished from start to finish by ʰfaith. As the Scriptures say, "It is through ʰfaith that a righteous person has life."

2. THE HEART OF THE GOSPEL: JUSTIFICATION BY FAITH (1:18–4:25)
All Persons are Accountable to God for Sin (1:18-32)

¹⁸But God shows his ⁱanger from heaven against all sinful, wicked people who suppress the truth by their wickedness. ¹⁹They know the truth about God because he has made it obvious to them. ²⁰For ever since the world was created, people have seen the earth and sky. Through everything God made, they can clearly see his invisible qualities—his eternal power and divine nature. So they have no excuse for not knowing God.

1:9 When Paul uses the phrase *with all my heart* (or *in my spirit*), he might be describing the influence of God's Holy Spirit on his own inner person. The word *spirit* also refers to the deepest part of a person, which the phrase *all my heart* expresses well.

1:11 *some spiritual gift:* Paul is probably referring to the spiritual benefit that he hopes his ministry will *bring* to the Roman Christians.

1:13 *brothers and sisters* (literally *brothers*): This Greek word (*adelphoi*) describes people who are in a familial relationship. Paul and other NT writers use this word to indicate that Christians are so intimately tied to one another in Christ that they are family. The word refers to both male and female Christians. • *I was prevented until now:* Paul wrote this letter when he was in Corinth toward the end of his third missionary journey (see Acts 20:2-4; cp. Rom 16:21-23). The need to plant and nourish churches in the eastern Mediterranean had occupied Paul up to this point. Before he could visit the Roman Christians, he first needed to return to Jerusalem to deliver a gift of money collected from the Gentile churches for the impoverished Jewish Christians (15:23-29).

1:14 *to people in both the civilized world and the rest of the world* (literally *to Greeks and barbarians*): The Greeks prided themselves on being sophisticated and cultured,

while regarding people from other cultures as inferior. They mocked other peoples' poorly spoken Greek, claiming that they could only say "bar bar," a nonsense phrase from which our word *barbarian* comes. Paul uses this cultural divide to emphasize his intention to preach the Good News to all kinds of people.

1:16 Paul consistently emphasizes that the Good News is for *everyone*. He also insists that God *first* chose the Jews to be his people, made promises to them, and gave them a unique place in the continuing plan of God (3:1-8; 9:1-5). They have a special responsibility to respond to the Good News and will be judged first if they turn away (2:9-10). • *also the Gentile:* Literally *also the Greek.*

1:17 *how God makes us right in his sight* (literally *the righteousness of God*): This key phrase appears eight times in Romans (see also 3:5, 21, 22, 25, 26; 10:3; the only other occurrence in Paul's writings is 2 Cor 5:21). The expression has OT roots, where God's righteousness refers to his character (as holy or faithful) or to an act of declaring his people sinless and perfect in his eyes (see especially Isa 46:13; 51:5-8). Paul uses the second meaning in this verse. The Good News has the power to save because it is the fulfillment of God's promise to vindicate his people. • The phrase *makes us right* comes from the law court. It does not mean

"makes us good people"; it means "puts us in right standing before God." • *"It is through faith that a righteous person has life"* (or *"The righteous will live by faith"* Hab 2:4): The prophet Habakkuk had struggled to understand how God could use pagan nations to judge his own people Israel. God reminded Habakkuk that his true people—the *righteous*—need to live by faith. In chs 1–4, Paul repeatedly insists that only through faith can human beings be made right in God's sight.

1:18–3:20 Paul delays exploring the theme of righteousness through faith (see 3:21) until he first teaches about universal sinfulness. Gentiles (1:18-32) and Jews (2:1–3:8) are equally under sin's power and cannot find favor with God by any action of their own (3:9-20).

1:18 God's *anger* is not a spontaneous emotional outburst, but the holy God's necessary response to sin. The OT often depicts God's anger (Exod 32:10-12; Num 11:1; Jer 21:3-7) and predicts a decisive outpouring of God's wrath on human sin at the end of history. While Paul usually depicts God's anger as occurring in the end times (2:5, 8; 5:9; Col 3:6; 1 Thes 1:10), the present tense of *shows* refers to God's expressions of anger throughout human history. • *who suppress the truth by their wickedness:* Or *who, by their wickedness, prevent the truth from being known.*

²¹Yes, they knew God, but they wouldn't worship him as God or even give him thanks. And they began to think up foolish ideas of what God was like. As a result, their minds became dark and confused. ²²Claiming to be wise, they instead became utter fools. ²³And instead of worshiping the glorious, ever-living God, they worshiped idols made to look like mere people and birds and animals and reptiles.

²⁴So God abandoned them to do whatever shameful things their hearts desired. As a result, they did vile and degrading things with each other's bodies. ²⁵They traded the truth about God for a lie. So they worshiped and served the things God created instead of the Creator himself, who is worthy of eternal praise! Amen. ²⁶That is why God abandoned them to their shameful desires. Even the women turned against the natural way to have sex and instead indulged in sex with each other. ²⁷And the men, instead of having normal sexual relations with women, burned with lust for each other. Men did shameful things with other men, and as a result of this sin, they suffered within themselves the penalty they deserved.

²⁸Since they thought it foolish to acknowledge God, he abandoned them to their foolish thinking and let them do things that should never be done. ²⁹Their lives became full of every kind of wickedness, sin, greed, hate, envy, murder, quarreling, deception, malicious behavior, and gossip. ³⁰They are backstabbers, haters of God, insolent, proud, and boastful. They invent new ways of sinning, and they disobey their parents. ³¹They refuse to understand, break their promises, are heartless, and have no mercy. ³²They know God's justice requires that those who do these things deserve to die, yet they do them anyway. Worse yet, they encourage others to do them, too.

Jews are Accountable to God for Sin (2:1–3:8)

The Jews and the Judgment of God

2 You may think you can condemn such people, but you are just as bad, and you have no excuse! When you say they are wicked and should be punished, you are condemning yourself, for you who judge others do these very same things. ²And we know that God, in his justice, will punish anyone who does such things. ³Since you judge others for doing these things, why do you think you can avoid God's judgment when you do the same things? ⁴Don't you see how wonderfully kind, tolerant, and patient God is with you? Does this mean nothing to you? Can't you see that his kindness is intended to ʲturn you from your sin?

⁵But because you are stubborn and refuse to turn from your sin, you are storing up ᵏterrible punishment for yourself. For a day of ᵏanger is coming, when God's righteous judgment will be revealed. ⁶He will judge everyone according to what they have

1:21
2 Kgs 17:15
Eph 4:17-18

1:22
Jer 10:14
1 Cor 1:20

1:23
Deut 4:15-19
Ps 106:20

1:24
Acts 14:16

1:26
1 Thes 4:5

1:27
Lev 18:22; 20:13
1 Cor 6:9

1:30
2 Tim 3:2

1:31
2 Tim 3:3

1:32
Rom 6:23

2:1
Matt 7:1

2:4
Rom 9:22
2 Pet 3:9, 15
ʲmetanoia (3341)
▸ 2 Tim 2:25

2:5
Ps 110:5
ᵏorgē (3709)
▸ Rom 2:8

2:6
*Ps 62:12
Matt 16:27

2:7
Matt 25:46
2 Tim 4:14

1:21 To *know God* in Scripture usually means to have an intimate, saving relationship with him (see 2 Cor 5:16; Gal 4:9; Phil 3:8, 10). Here, however, *they knew God* means that people knew about God. All people have some understanding of God through creation, yet they do not do what is right based on that knowledge. Rather than learn more about God, they worship gods of their own making.

1:24 When human beings exchanged the living God for idols, God *abandoned them,* a point Paul makes twice more in this paragraph (1:26, 28). The word *abandon* includes a sense of "handing over," suggesting that God actively consigns people to the consequences of their sin.

1:26 *women turned against the natural way:* In this context, *natural way* refers to the nature of the world as God made it. As in the OT, Paul singles out homosexuality as a key illustration of how people have fallen away from worship of the true God (see Gen 19:1-28; Lev 18:22; 20:13; Deut 23:17-18). God created human beings as male and female, and engaging in homosexual activity is a violation of God's creative intention.

1:27 *suffered within themselves the penalty they deserved:* When people abandon the Creator's intentions, they are judged for their actions. This judgment can take many different forms, but the ultimate consequence is spiritual death (see 1:32).

1:28 *thought it foolish:* Sin affects our actions and even our thoughts. One of the serious consequences of turning away from God is an unsound mind; people can no longer use their minds as God intended.

1:29-31 This list of sins follows a popular Hellenistic literary form called a *vice list.* While not exhaustive, it reminds readers of various forms that evil might take.

1:32 To *encourage others* to sin is *worse* than sinning oneself (Jas 3:1; cp. *Testament of Asher* 6:2: "The two-faced are doubly punished because they both practice evil and approve of others who practice it; they imitate the spirits of error and join in the struggle against mankind").

2:1-5 *You* is singular in the Greek. Here, the *you* is a hypothetical complacent Jew, who feels superior to Gentiles and in no danger of judgment. Paul adopts a popular Hellenistic style called a *diatribe,* in which a writer tries to win over an audience to his views by portraying a debate between himself and a hypothetical opponent. • *these very same things:* Paul's point is that Jews, like Gentiles, turn from God's revelation to go their own way.

2:4 *Can't you see that his kindness is intended to turn you from your sin?* Behind Paul's question are Jewish passages (e.g., *Wisdom of Solomon* 12–15; cp. Jer 7:1-5; Amos 5:18-27) that portray a prevalent Jewish complacency toward judgment. Many Jews thought that because they were God's people, they did not need to worry about judgment, for their sins would not be punished as the sins of Gentiles would be. Paul emphasizes that God's grace was intended to turn the Jews from their sin, not to condone a sinful lifestyle.

2:6-11 Paul uses a *chiasm* ("X" arrangement) to make his point:

2:8
2 Thes 2:12
ᵃorgē (3709)
▸ Eph 2:3

2:11
Gal 2:6
Eph 6:9
Col 3:25

2:12
ᵇnomos (3551)
▸ Rom 7:7

2:13
Matt 7:21
John 13:17
Jas 1:22-25

2:14
Acts 10:35

2:16
Acts 10:42
Rom 16:25
2 Tim 2:8
ᶜeuangelion (2098)
▸ Rom 15:19

2:17
Mic 3:11

done. 7He will give eternal life to those who keep on doing good, seeking after the glory and honor and immortality that God offers. 8But he will pour out his ᵃanger and wrath on those who live for themselves, who refuse to obey the truth and instead live lives of wickedness. 9There will be trouble and calamity for everyone who keeps on doing what is evil—for the Jew first and also for the Gentile. 10But there will be glory and honor and peace from God for all who do good—for the Jew first and also for the Gentile. 11For God does not show favoritism.

12When the Gentiles sin, they will be destroyed, even though they never had God's written law. And the Jews, who do have God's ᵇlaw, will be judged by that ᵇlaw when they fail to obey it. 13For merely listening to the law doesn't make us right with God. It is obeying the law that makes us right in his sight. 14Even Gentiles, who do not have God's written law, show that they know his law when they instinctively obey it, even without having heard it. 15They demonstrate that God's law is written in their hearts, for their own conscience and thoughts either accuse them or tell them they are doing right. 16And this is the ᶜmessage I proclaim—that the day is coming when God, through Christ Jesus, will judge everyone's secret life.

The Limitations of the Covenant
17You who call yourselves Jews are relying on God's law, and you boast about your special relationship with him. 18You know what

Natural Revelation (1:19-21)

Ps 19:1-4
Acts 14:15-17;
17:24-29

When God speaks to people directly through his word, we call it *special revelation*. God also speaks to all people indirectly in *natural revelation,* through the world of nature he has created. Psalm 19, for example, proclaims that knowledge of God in creation is universal (see Ps 19:1-4).

Sadly, however, a saving response to God is anything but universal. Paul teaches in Romans 1–3 that as a result of Adam's sin, all people turn away from the knowledge of God that they find in the created world. Apart from God's grace, natural revelation only condemns people; as Paul states in 1:20, "They have no excuse for not knowing God."

God can still use natural revelation to awaken people to the reality of the one true God. When accompanied and empowered by the grace of God, the beauty and intricacy of the world can stimulate a search for the Creator. Paul appealed to natural revelation in Athens (Acts 17:16-31) as a bridge to preaching the Good News. God's revelation in the natural world and in human nature can stimulate people to search for the true God. And then, through the special revelation he has given in Scripture and in his Son, Jesus Christ, people can come to know him and experience his salvation.

A God judges everyone the same (2:6)
  B Life is the reward for doing good (2:7)
    C Wrath is the penalty for evil (2:8)
    C' Wrath for doing evil (2:9)
  B' Life for doing good (2:10)
A' God shows no favoritism (2:11)

2:7 *He will give eternal life to those who keep on doing good:* Paul makes it clear elsewhere that no one can receive eternal life except as God's gift through faith (3:20, 28; 4:1-8). Here, Paul is either referring to Christians whose good deeds (that result from faith) will be taken into account in God's judgment, or he is reminding readers of the absolute standard that God's own holiness establishes, since only by perfection can sinners hope to find acceptance before God. As the argument of the letter unfolds, Paul will show that no one is capable of meeting that standard.

2:8 *Live for themselves* translates a rare Greek word (*eritheia*) that seems to convey the idea of selfish ambition or strife.

Using this word, Aristotle scolded the politicians of his day for seeking public office for selfish gain rather than from a desire to serve the people (Aristotle, *Politics* 5.3; see also 2 Cor 12:20; Gal 5:20; Phil 1:17; 2:3; Jas 3:14, 16).

2:9 *also for the Gentile:* Literally *also for the Greek;* also in 2:10.

2:12 *destroyed:* This common NT word describes the fate of the wicked after death (see also 9:22; 14:15; 1 Cor 1:18; 15:18; 2 Cor 2:15; 4:3; Phil 1:28; 3:19; 2 Thes 2:10; 1 Tim 6:9). Condemned sinners do not cease to exist, but they suffer eternal punishment, which includes the everlasting destruction of all good in their identity and experience. • *the Jews, who do have God's law:* The Jews were given the law of Moses, while the Gentiles *never had God's written law.* In the NT period, Jews emphasized their possession of the law as a mark of God's favor and even as a guarantee of salvation.

2:13 *obeying the law . . . makes us right in his sight:* Regarding the promise of

righteousness through obedience, see 2:7; see also Jas 1:22.

2:14-15 The *Gentiles* who *know his law when they instinctively obey it* may be Gentile Christians, especially since *written in their hearts* (2:15) alludes to the prophecy of the new covenant (Jer 31:31-34). Or they could be non-Christian Gentiles who know God's general moral law through their consciences. In this case, Paul would be using the notion of *natural law* to show how all people could be held accountable for certain basic moral requirements.

2:16 *secret life* (literally *the hidden things*): Scripture frequently stresses that God will judge people according to their thoughts and intentions (see 1 Sam 16:7; Ps 139:1-2; Jer 17:10).

2:17-20 The boasting of the *Jews* reflects OT and Jewish teaching about the privileges and responsibilities God gave to Israel. God gave *his law* to Israel, entered into a *special relationship* with them, and commissioned them to be *a light* to the Gentiles (see Isa 42:6-7).

he wants; you know what is right because you have been taught his law. ¹⁹You are convinced that you are a guide for the blind and a light for people who are lost in darkness. ²⁰You think you can instruct the ignorant and teach children the ways of God. For you are certain that God's law gives you complete knowledge and truth.

²¹Well then, if you teach others, why don't you teach yourself? You tell others not to steal, but do you steal? ²²You say it is wrong to commit adultery, but do you commit adultery? You condemn idolatry, but do you use items stolen from pagan temples? ²³You are so proud of knowing the law, but you dishonor God by breaking it. ²⁴No wonder the Scriptures say, "The Gentiles blaspheme the name of God because of you."

²⁵The Jewish ceremony of circumcision has value only if you obey God's law. But if you don't obey God's law, you are no better off than an uncircumcised Gentile. ²⁶And if the Gentiles obey God's law, won't God declare them to be his own people? ²⁷In fact, uncircumcised Gentiles who keep God's law will condemn you Jews who are circumcised and possess God's law but don't obey it.

²⁸For you are not a true Jew just because you were born of Jewish parents or because you have gone through the ceremony of circumcision. ²⁹No, a true Jew is one whose heart is right with God. And true circumcision is not merely obeying the letter of the law; rather, it is a change of heart produced by God's Spirit. And a person with a changed heart seeks praise from God, not from people.

God's Faithfulness and the Judgment of Jews

3 Then what's the advantage of being a Jew? Is there any value in the ceremony of circumcision? ²Yes, there are great benefits! First of all, the Jews were entrusted with the whole revelation of God.

³True, some of them were unfaithful; but just because they were unfaithful, does that mean God will be unfaithful? ⁴Of course not! Even if everyone else is a liar, God is true. As the Scriptures say about him,

"You will be proved right in what you say,
    and you will win your case in court."

⁵"But," some might say, "our sinfulness serves a good purpose, for it helps people see how righteous God is. Isn't it unfair,

2:20
2 Tim 3:5
2:21
Matt 23:3-4
2:24
*Isa 52:5
Ezek 36:20
2:25
Gal 5:3
2:28
Matt 3:9
John 8:39
Gal 6:15
2:29
Deut 30:6
John 5:44
Rom 7:6
2 Cor 3:6; 10:18
Phil 3:3
Col 2:11
1 Pet 3:4
3:2
Deut 4:7-8
Ps 147:19-20
Acts 7:38
3:4
*Ps 51:4
3:5
Rom 5:8

. . . .

Jews were not wrong to enjoy these blessings; their error was in failing to live up to their privileged position.

2:21-22 Paul again uses the diatribe style to expose the inconsistency of Jewish claims (see note on 2:1-5).

2:22 *do you use items stolen from pagan temples?* (literally *do you steal from temples?*): OT law prohibited Jews from having anything to do with pagan idols (see Deut 7:26), but first-century Jews did not strictly follow this law. Sometimes they stole idols and used or sold the precious metals.

2:24 Paul quotes Isa 52:5 (Greek version), where God's *name* is blasphemed because Israel is oppressed by pagan nations. Here, Paul uses that passage to demonstrate the failure of the Jews to live up to their responsibilities.

2:25 God instituted *the Jewish ceremony of circumcision* as a sign of his covenant with Abraham; it was to be performed on every male Israelite child (Gen 17:9-13; see Rom 4:11). Circumcision therefore represents God's covenant with his people Israel. The rite took on greater significance during the intertestamental period when the pagan king Antiochus IV Epiphanes tried to stamp out the Jewish faith by forbidding circumcision. The Jews resisted in the famous Maccabean Revolt (166–160 BC). After they restored the worship of the Lord in Israel, the Jews regarded circumcision as a highly

prized mark of Jewish loyalty in the midst of a pagan culture.

2:26 *won't God declare them to be his own people?* Paul might be speaking of Gentile Christians who are God's people because they obey God's law, or he could be speaking hypothetically about what would happen if a Gentile perfectly obeyed God's law.

2:29 *The letter of the law* refers to the law of God written on tablets of stone (see 2 Cor 3:3), while *God's Spirit* now writes his law on people's hearts (Jer 31:33-34). Outward conformity is thus contrasted with obedience motivated by *a change of heart.* • *seeks praise:* Or *receives praise.*

3:1 *what's the advantage of being a Jew?* Paul moves his argument along by raising questions. After preaching the Good News for over twenty years, he knew what questions people would ask when they heard a particular teaching. His emphasis on the equality of Jews and Gentiles before God (ch 2) inevitably led people to ask whether he was eliminating all Jewish privileges. The question-and-answer style follows the pattern of the diatribe (see note on 2:1-5).

3:2 The advantage that Jews possessed was in having received God's word.
• *First of all:* Paul never adds a second or a third point to the list he begins here. He might have forgotten to continue the list, or *first of all* might mean

"most importantly." However, 9:4-5 provides a good indication of what a list of Jewish privileges would have included.
• *the whole revelation of God* (literally *the oracles of God*): By using the word *oracles* (Greek *logia*), Paul highlights God's personal communication with his people (see Deut 33:9; Ps 105:19) through which he gives them special privileges and responsibilities.

3:4 *Of course not!* The Greek *mē genoito* is an emphatic negation, popular in the diatribe style that Paul uses here and in several other passages in Romans (see 3:6, 31; 6:2, 15; 7:7, 13; 9:14; 11:1, 11).
• *As the Scriptures say:* Paul quotes Ps 51:4 (Greek version), where David confessed his sin in having an adulterous relationship with Bathsheba (see 2 Sam 11). God punished David, and David admitted that God was *proved right* and would *win* his *case in court*—his punishment was entirely just. God is faithful to what he has said in the past—his entire revelation—and his words warn of punishment for sin even as they promise reward for obedience.

3:5-7 *how would he be qualified to judge the world?* Abraham asked a similar question: "Should not the Judge of all the earth do what is right?" (Gen 18:25). God punishes all sin, and he retains absolute righteousness as he does so. Even when God makes use of human sin for his own ends, that sin still deserves to be, and will be, punished (see 9:10-24).

3:7
Rom 9:19

3:8
Rom 6:1

3:9
Rom 1:18–2:24
ᵈ*hamartia* (0266)
  ▸ Rom 4:7

3:10-12
*Ps 14:1-3; 53:1-3

3:13
*Ps 5:9; 140:3

3:14
*Ps 10:7

3:15-17
*Isa 59:7-8

3:18
*Ps 36:1

3:19
Rom 2:12

3:20
Ps 143:2
Rom 4:15; 7:7
Gal 2:16; 3:11

3:21
Gen 15:6
Rom 1:2, 17; 9:30
ᵉ*dikaiosunē* (1343)
  ▸ Rom 4:3

3:22
Rom 4:11; 10:4, 12
Gal 2:16
Col 3:11
ᶠ*pisteuō* (4100)
  ▸ Rom 3:25

then, for him to punish us?" (This is merely a human point of view.) 6Of course not! If God were not entirely fair, how would he be qualified to judge the world? 7"But," someone might still argue, "how can God condemn me as a sinner if my dishonesty highlights his truthfulness and brings him more glory?" 8And some people even slander us by claiming that we say, "The more we sin, the better it is!" Those who say such things deserve to be condemned.

The Guilt of All Humanity (3:9-20)

9Well then, should we conclude that we Jews are better than others? No, not at all, for we have already shown that all people, whether Jews or Gentiles, are under the power of ᵈsin. 10As the Scriptures say,

"No one is righteous—
    not even one.
11 No one is truly wise;
    no one is seeking God.
12 All have turned away;
    all have become useless.
No one does good,
    not a single one."
13 "Their talk is foul, like the stench from
    an open grave.

Their tongues are filled with lies."
"Snake venom drips from their lips."
14 "Their mouths are full of cursing and
    bitterness."
15 "They rush to commit murder.
16 Destruction and misery always follow
    them.
17 They don't know where to find
    peace."
18 "They have no fear of God at all."

19Obviously, the law applies to those to whom it was given, for its purpose is to keep people from having excuses, and to show that the entire world is guilty before God. 20For no one can ever be made right with God by doing what the law commands. The law simply shows us how sinful we are.

Justification and the Righteousness of God (3:21-26)

21But now God has shown us a way to be made ᵉright with him without keeping the requirements of the law, as was promised in the writings of Moses and the prophets long ago. 22We are made right with God by placing our faith in Jesus Christ. And this is true for everyone who ᶠbelieves, no matter who we are.

3:8 *some people even slander us:* Paul is referring to misrepresentations about his teaching on justification by faith. If a person is made right with God by faith alone, through God's grace and apart from works, it could seem as if the Good News allows believers to sin because their sin is forgiven when confessed (see 6:1). One of Paul's purposes is to help the Roman Christians understand that such misunderstandings are without basis.

3:9 *No, not at all:* Paul's emphatic answer does not contradict his claim in 3:1-2 that Jews have an advantage. But that advantage has not done them any good because they have disobeyed God's word and incurred God's punishment. Jews, like Gentiles, have sinned against the revelation of God and stand condemned. • *under the power of sin* (literally *under sin*): Being "under" something carries the sense of being under its power. The ultimate problem of human beings is not the fact of sin, but the more basic situation of being slaves to sin. The solution to this problem requires the liberation provided in Christ Jesus, who frees us from both the penalty and the power of sin.

3:10-18 The five quotations in these verses, drawn from various parts of the OT, all address human sinfulness. Paul follows the practice of rabbis who gathered together OT texts on similar themes in a practice called *pearl-stringing.*

3:10-12 This quotation from Ps 14:1-3; 53:1-3 (Greek version) directly supports the argument that all people are under the power of sin.

3:13-14 Paul here refers to sins of speech, mentioning a different organ of speech in each of the four lines (**talk** in 3:13 is literally *throat*).

3:13 These quotations are from Ps 5:9 (Greek version); 140:3.

3:14 This quotation is from Ps 10:7 (Greek version).

3:15-17 In this quotation from Isa 59:7-8, Paul addresses sins against others.

3:18 This concluding quotation from Ps 36:1 neatly ties up the whole series (3:10-18) by referring to the same Greek words that introduced the first quotation (*ouk estin,* "they have no" and "no one is").

3:19 Paul speaks of the entire OT as *the law* (see also 1 Cor 9:8, 9; 14:21, 34; Gal 4:21). • *Those to whom it was given* (literally *those in the law*) were the Jews, who were given the Scriptures. • How can Paul conclude that *the entire world is guilty before God* on the basis of evidence from the OT that Jews are sinful? He argues "from the greater to the lesser": If the law shows that the Jews, God's own people, are guilty, then how much more are the Gentiles, who have

not had the benefit of God's instruction, also guilty.

3:20 *By doing what the law commands* refers to obeying the requirements of the law of Moses. While this phrase refers to Jews, the principle extends to all people. If Jews cannot be put in right relationship with God by obeying the law God gave them, certainly other people cannot establish such a relationship through good deeds.

3:21–4:25 Paul returns to the central theme of the *righteousness* of God that is revealed in Christ and is available to anyone who believes. The fundamental statement of this theology is in 3:21-26; Paul elaborates on it in 3:27-31, and illustrates it with the experience of Abraham in ch 4.

3:21-22 After a lengthy reminder of the power of sin (1:18–3:20), Paul returns to the theme presented in 1:17, the *way to be made right with* God (literally *the righteousness of God*). As in that verse, "the righteousness of God" is the way that God puts people in right relationship with himself. • *without keeping the requirements of the law* (literally *apart from the law*): The old covenant looked forward to the climactic revelation of God's righteousness in his Son. What God now accomplishes for us in Christ, he does apart from the covenant structure set up by the law of Moses (Heb 8:13). • *the writings of Moses:* Literally *the law.*

²³For everyone has sinned; we all fall short of God's ᵍglorious standard. ²⁴Yet God, with undeserved ʰkindness, declares that we are righteous. He did this through Christ Jesus when he ⁱfreed us from the penalty for our sins. ²⁵For God presented Jesus as the ʲsacrifice for sin. People are made right with God when they ᵏbelieve that Jesus sacrificed his life, shedding his blood. This sacrifice shows that God was being fair when he held back and did not punish those who sinned in times past, ²⁶for he was looking ahead and including them in what he would do in this present time. God did this to demonstrate his righteousness, for he himself is fair and just, and he declares sinners to be right in his sight when they believe in Jesus.

Justification "By Faith Alone" (3:27–4:25)
"By Faith Alone": Initial Statement
²⁷Can we boast, then, that we have done anything to be accepted by God? No, because our acquittal is not based on obeying the law. It is based on faith. ²⁸So we are made right with God through faith and not by obeying the law.

²⁹After all, is God the God of the Jews only? Isn't he also the God of the Gentiles? Of course he is. ³⁰There is only one God, and he makes people right with himself only by faith, whether they are Jews or Gentiles. ³¹Well then, if we emphasize faith, does this mean that we can forget about the law? Of course not! In fact, only when we have faith do we truly fulfill the law.

"By Faith Alone": Abraham
4 Abraham was, humanly speaking, the founder of our Jewish nation. What did he discover about being made right with God? ²If his good deeds had made him acceptable to God, he would have had something to boast about. But that was not God's way. ³For the Scriptures tell us, "Abraham believed God, and God counted him as ªrighteous because of his faith."

⁴When people work, their wages are not a gift, but something they have earned. ⁵But people are counted as righteous, not because of their work, but because of their faith in God who forgives sinners. ⁶David also spoke of this when he described the happiness of those who are declared righteous without working for it:

⁷ "Oh, what ᵇjoy for those
    whose disobedience is forgiven,
    whose ᶜsins are put out of sight.

3:23
ᵉdoxa (1391)
▸ 1 Cor 11:7

3:24
Eph 2:8
Heb 9:12
ʰcharis (5485)
▸ Rom 5:2
ⁱapolutrōsis (0629)
▸ Rom 8:23

3:25
Lev 16:10
Heb 9:12-14
1 Pet 1:19
1 Jn 4:10
ʲhilastērion (2435)
▸ Heb 2:17
ᵏpistis (4102)
▸ Rom 5:1

3:27
Rom 2:17; 4:2
1 Cor 1:29-31

3:28
Acts 13:39

3:29
Rom 10:12
Gal 3:28

3:31
Matt 5:17

4:2
1 Cor 1:31

4:3
ªGen 15:6
Gal 3:6
Jas 2:23
ªdikaiosunē (1343)
▸ Rom 4:9

4:4
Rom 11:6
Gal 2:16

3:24 *undeserved kindness:* God *declares that we are righteous,* not because he has to, but because he has freely chosen to give us his favor *through Christ Jesus.* Because we are helpless slaves of sin (3:9), our righteous status before God can never be earned (see 4:4-5). • *through Christ Jesus when he freed us from the penalty for our sins* (literally *through the redemption that is in Christ Jesus*): In Paul's day, *redemption* referred to the price paid to free a slave. God paid our redemption price with the blood of his own Son to rescue us from our slavery to sin (see 3:9). This language was used in the OT to refer to the Exodus, the first redemption of God's people from bondage (see 2 Sam 7:23). God promised that he would again redeem his people (Hos 13:14; Mic 4:10).

3:25 *the sacrifice for sin* (Greek *hilastērion*): This Greek word is used in the Greek OT to refer to the "atonement cover," the cover that rested on the Ark of the Covenant in the inner sanctuary of the Tabernacle. The atonement cover was prominent in the Day of Atonement ritual (Lev 16) and came to stand for the atonement ceremony itself. Paul characterizes Jesus Christ as God's provision of final atonement for his people. Jesus himself satisfies, or absorbs in himself, the anger of God against all sinful people (see 1:18). • *those who*

sinned in times past: Paul refers to righteous OT people who were not punished for their sins as strict justice would require. Hebrews reminds us, "it is not possible for the blood of bulls and goats to take away sins" (Heb 10:4). How, then, could God forgive people in the OT? Paul answers that Jesus' sacrifice works backward in history as well as forward—through Christ, God provided for the full satisfaction of his righteous anger against human sin.

3:29-30 Paul uses the foundational Jewish commitment to monotheism to argue for universal access to God's forgiveness. If *there is only one God,* then he is equally the God of both Jews and Gentiles. All people must be able to come to God on the same terms, through *faith.* • *whether they are Jews or Gentiles:* Literally *whether they are circumcised or uncircumcised.*

3:31 *we truly fulfill the law:* Paul knows that some people will object to his insistence on faith apart from the law because it seems to dismiss the demands of the law. However, *faith* actually enables people to *fulfill the law.* The Holy Spirit is given to those who have faith, and he makes it possible for people to do as they should.

4:1 Jews in Paul's day revered *Abraham* as Israel's *founder.* Some Jewish texts claim that Abraham never sinned

(*Prayer of Manasseh* 8; *Jubilees* 23:10). Others emphasize his obedience to the law of Moses as the basis for his relationship with God (*1 Maccabees* 2:52; *Sirach* 44:19-20). However, Paul demonstrates that Abraham's faith, not his obedience, established his status with God. Abraham's position as the founder of God's people demonstrates that justification by faith is central in God's plan.

4:3 Paul quotes Gen 15:6. In response to God's promise that he would have descendants as numerous as the stars in the sky, *Abraham believed God.* It was faith that established Abraham's relationship with God—not works (4:3-8), circumcision (4:9-12), the law (4:13-17), or the number of his descendants (4:18-21).

4:4-5 The logic of these verses is as follows: (1) The stated premise is that *when people work,* their pay is what *they have earned,* not a gift. (2) The unstated premise is that God is never indebted to his creatures (because they owe him everything), so anything he gives them is *a gift* (see also 9:14-16). (3) The conclusion is that therefore, people cannot be declared *righteous* before God because of their works.

4:7-8 This quotation from Ps 32:1-2 (Greek version) follows the Jewish custom of supporting a reference to the

4:7-8
*Ps 32:1-2
2 Cor 5:19
ᵇmakarios (3107)
▸ Titus 2:13
ᶜhamartia (0266)
▸ Rom 5:12

4:9
Gen 15:6
Rom 3:30
ᵈdikaiosunē (1343)
▸ Rom 5:17

4:11
Gen 17:10-11
ᵉpatēr (3962)
▸ 1 Cor 1:3

4:13
Gen 18:18; 22:17-18
Gal 3:29

4:14
Gal 3:18

4:15
Rom 3:20; 7:12
1 Cor 15:55-56
Gal 3:10

4:16
Gal 3:7

⁸ Yes, what ᵇjoy for those
    whose record the Lᴏʀᴅ has cleared
       of ᶜsin."

⁹Now, is this blessing only for the Jews, or is it also for uncircumcised Gentiles? Well, we have been saying that Abraham was counted as ᵈrighteous by God because of his faith. ¹⁰But how did this happen? Was he counted as righteous only after he was circumcised, or was it before he was circumcised? Clearly, God accepted Abraham before he was circumcised!

¹¹Circumcision was a sign that Abraham already had faith and that God had already accepted him and declared him to be righteous—even before he was circumcised. So Abraham is the spiritual ᵉfather of those who have faith but have not been circumcised. They are counted as righteous because of their faith. ¹²And Abraham is also the spiritual father of those who have been circumcised, but only if they have the same kind of faith Abraham had before he was circumcised.

¹³Clearly, God's promise to give the whole earth to Abraham and his descendants was based not on his obedience to God's law, but on a right relationship with God that comes by faith. ¹⁴If God's promise is only for those who obey the law, then faith is not necessary and the promise is pointless. ¹⁵For the law always brings punishment on those who try to obey it. (The only way to avoid breaking the law is to have no law to break!)

¹⁶So the promise is received by faith. It is given as a free gift. And we are all certain

God's Unified Plan of Salvation (3:21-26)

Rom 1:3-5, 16-17;
5:6-11; 8:1-4; 10:5-
13; 11:26-27
Matt 1:21-23
Luke 1:46-55, 67-79
Acts 4:10-12; 10:34-
43; 13:23-41
1 Cor 15:1-4
Gal 2:14-21; 3:5-14
Eph 1:3-14
Col 1:15-22
1 Tim 2:3-6
2 Tim 1:9-10
Heb 9:27-28

The continuity of God's unfolding plan of salvation is a central theme in Romans. In 3:21, Paul makes two important points about the new way of being "made right" with God that has been inaugurated in Jesus Christ. First, it does not depend on obeying the laws and regulations of the OT. Second, it was "promised in the writings of Moses and the prophets" (3:21). God has always planned to save the world through Jesus, and the entire OT was a preparation for that climactic moment in salvation history. In 1:2, Paul claims that "God promised this Good News long ago through his prophets in the holy Scriptures." Paul keeps returning to this theme of continuity, especially in chs 9–11, where he shows how God's dealings with Israel fit into that single, unfolding plan.

At the same time, Paul is also concerned to help us understand the discontinuity in God's single plan of salvation. That plan unfolds in stages. Now that the final stage in Christ has arrived, the prior stage—during which the law of Moses ruled over God's people—has been left behind. Paul repeatedly emphasizes that our new relationship with God stands separate from the law of Moses (see 6:14, 15; 7:4-6; 10:4). A similar point is made in John 1:17 and Heb 10:1. Paul's recurring focus in Romans on the nature of God's plan helps us to put the whole story of the Bible together in a way that honors both of its parts.

Law with a reference in the Prophets or the Writings. Paul also uses a Jewish exegetical technique of linking unrelated quotations with a key word. Here, *record . . . has cleared* translates the same Greek word as "counted" in 4:3.

4:9 *is this blessing only for the Jews, or is it also for uncircumcised Gentiles?* Literally *is this blessing only for the circumcised, or is it also for the uncircumcised?*

4:10 *God accepted Abraham before he was circumcised!* Paul's point is simple: God's declaration of Abraham's righteousness in Gen 15:6 could not have been based on his circumcision, which happened later (Gen 17). This point further demonstrates that God's acceptance and blessing is a free gift and not earned by works.

4:11-12 When God instituted circumcision, he called it *"a sign* of the covenant" between himself and Abraham (Gen

17:11). The covenant was *already* in place (Gen 12:1-3; 15:1-21; 17:1-8) *even before* Abraham *was circumcised* (Gen 17:9-14). This shows that the covenant was based on faith, not circumcision. *So Abraham is the spiritual father* of all people, whether *circumcised* (Jews) or uncircumcised (Gentiles), who *have the same kind of faith Abraham had*—that is, faith in God's promises (4:13-25).

4:13 *the whole earth:* God told Abraham that he would be the father of many nations (4:17; Gen 12:2; 13:16; 15:5; 17:4-6, 16-20; 22:17) and that he would be the means of blessing to all people (Gen 12:3; 18:18; 22:18; cp. Isa 55:3-5).

4:14 *then faith is not necessary* (literally *faith is emptied*): If works of obedience can be substituted for faith, then "faith is emptied" of its importance. Believing in God means acknowledging our unworthiness and depending entirely on God's mercy.

4:15 *The only way to avoid breaking the law is to have no law to break!* (literally *where there is no law, neither is there transgression*): Paul always uses the word "transgression" to denote disobedience of a clear commandment of God (see also 2:23; 5:14; Gal 3:19; 1 Tim 2:14). Transgression only exists where the law exists, which is why *the law always brings punishment*. The law that God gave to the Israelites specified requirements in great detail, which made the people more accountable for sin than before. So when they inevitably disobeyed the law, God brought more severe punishment upon them.

4:16 *whether or not we live according to the law of Moses* (literally *not only those who are of the law*): The Jews were *of the law* in that their covenant with God included the law of Moses and they were to live according to it.

to receive it, whether or not we live according to the law of Moses, if we have faith like Abraham's. For Abraham is the father of all who believe. [17]That is what the Scriptures mean when God told him, "I have made you the father of many nations." This happened because Abraham believed in the God who [f]brings the dead back to life and who creates new things out of nothing.

[18]Even when there was no reason for hope, Abraham kept hoping—believing that he would become the father of many nations. For God had said to him, "That's how many descendants you will have!" [19]And Abraham's faith did not weaken, even though, at about 100 years of age, he figured his body was as good as dead—and so was Sarah's womb.

[20]Abraham never wavered in believing God's promise. In fact, his faith grew stronger, and in this he brought glory to God. [21]He was fully convinced that God is able to do whatever he promises. [22]And because of Abraham's faith, God counted him as righteous. [23]And when God counted him as righteous, it wasn't just for Abraham's benefit. It was recorded [24]for our benefit, too, assuring us that God will also count us as righteous if we believe in him, the one who raised Jesus our Lord from the dead. [25]He was handed over to die because of our sins, and he was raised to life to make us [g]right with God.

3. THE ASSURANCE PROVIDED BY THE GOSPEL: THE HOPE OF SALVATION (5:1–8:39)

The Hope of Glory (5:1-21)

From Justification to Salvation

5 Therefore, since we have been made right in God's sight by [h]faith, we have [i]peace with God because of what Jesus Christ our Lord has done for us. [2]Because of our faith, Christ has brought us into this place of undeserved [j]privilege where we now stand, and we confidently and joyfully [k]look forward to sharing God's glory.

[3]We can rejoice, too, when we run into problems and trials, for we know that they help us develop endurance. [4]And endurance develops strength of character, and character strengthens our confident hope of salvation. [5]And this hope will not lead to disappointment. For we know how dearly God loves us, because he has given us the Holy Spirit to fill our hearts with his [a]love.

[6]When we were utterly helpless, Christ came at just the right time and died for us sinners. [7]Now, most people would not be willing to die for an upright person, though someone might perhaps be willing to die for a person who is especially good. [8]But God showed his great love for us by sending Christ to die for us while we were still sinners. [9]And since we have been made right in God's sight by the blood of Christ, he will certainly save us from God's condemnation.

4:17
*Gen 17:5
Isa 48:13
John 5:21
1 Cor 1:28
[i]*zōopoieō* (2227)
▸ Rom 8:11

4:18
*Gen 15:5

4:19
Gen 17:17; 18:11
Heb 11:11

4:22
*Gen 15:6
Rom 4:3

4:24
1 Pet 1:21

4:25
Isa 53:4-5
Rom 8:32
1 Cor 15:17
2 Cor 5:15
1 Pet 1:21
[g]*dikaiōsis* (1347)
▸ Rom 5:18

5:1
Acts 10:36
Rom 3:28
[h]*pistis* (4102)
▸ Rom 10:17
[i]*eirēnē* (1515)
▸ Rom 8:6

5:2
Eph 2:18; 3:12
[j]*charis* (5485)
▸ Rom 5:21
[k]*elpis* (1680)
▸ Rom 8:24

5:3
Matt 5:12
Jas 1:2-3

5:5
2 Cor 1:22
Gal 4:6
Eph 1:13
Phil 1:20
[a]*agapē* (0026)
▸ Rom 8:39

5:6
Gal 4:4
Eph 5:2

. . . .

4:17 This quotation is from Gen 17:5.

4:18 This quotation is from Gen 15:5.

4:24 *raised . . . from the dead:* Abraham experienced the life-giving power of God in the birth of his son, Isaac. Christians witness it in the resurrection of Jesus. Throughout history, salvation has been available only through faith in God, who makes and keeps his promises.

5:1–8:39 Paul now turns from the Good News about how people enter a relationship with God to the security of that relationship. Christians have a strong and unassailable promise because of God's work in Christ, God's love for them, and the power of the Holy Spirit. This theme frames the teaching of these chapters (5:1-11; 8:18-39) as Paul grounds that promise in the transfer of believers from the realm of Adam to the realm of Christ (5:12-21). No power—whether sin (ch 6), the law (ch 7), or death (8:1-13)—"will ever be able to separate us from the love of God" (8:39).

5:1 *we have peace:* In many manuscripts, the underlying Greek verb

is indicative, as translated here. A number of other manuscripts use the subjunctive instead (*let us have peace*). • *Peace with God* does not refer to a mere feeling of peacefulness but to a real situation of peace. It is the end of hostilities between God and sinful human beings when they believe in Jesus Christ and the state of blessing and salvation that God promised his people in the end (see Isa 9:6-7; 52:7; Ezek 34:25; Nah 1:15).

5:2 *undeserved privilege* (or *grace*): So basic is God's grace (Greek *charis*) that Paul can use the word to sum up our present situation as believers. • *Where we now stand* indicates that God's grace is needed throughout the Christian life, not just at the beginning. • *Sharing God's glory* describes the content of Christian hope, which Paul introduces here and expounds more fully in 8:18-30. Behind Paul's use of the word *glory* (Greek *doxa*) is the Hebrew word *kabod*, which depicts God's majesty and overwhelming presence (see "The Glory of God" at Exod 24:15-17, p. 167). The prophets predict a day when God's glory will return to dwell in the midst of his people (see, e.g., Isa 60:1-2).

5:3-4 See also Jas 1:2-4; 1 Pet 1:6-7. The similarities in these passages indicate early Christian teaching common to all three of these writers.

5:5 *this hope will not lead to disappointment* (literally *will not put to shame*): In the OT, shame sometimes refers to a negative verdict from God's judgment (e.g., Isa 28:16, quoted in Rom 9:33). • *he has given us the Holy Spirit to fill our hearts with his love:* See Jer 31:33-34; Acts 2:17-21.

5:6 *At just the right time* might mean that God sent Christ at the time appointed in history, or that our condition as *utterly helpless* was the right time for God to demonstrate his love by sending his Son on our behalf.

5:9 *The blood of Christ* refers to Jesus' sacrificial death (3:25). In the Scriptures, *blood* is shorthand for a violent death (Lev 17:11), especially when that death atones for sins. • *he will certainly save us from God's condemnation:* Paul frequently speaks of salvation as the final deliverance of believers from God's wrath and the tribulations of this life (see 13:11).

5:8
John 3:16
1 Jn 4:10

5:9
Rom 1:18; 2:5, 8

5:10
Rom 8:34
2 Cor 5:18-19
Eph 2:3
ᵇ*katallassō* (2644)
▸ Rom 5:11

5:11
ᶜ*katallagē* (2643)
▸ Rom 11:15

5:12
Gen 3:1-19
1 Cor 15:21-22
ᵈ*hamartia* (0266)
▸ Rom 6:1

5:14
ᵉ*tupos* (5179)
▸ 1 Cor 10:6

5:17
1 Cor 15:21
ᶠ*dikaiosunē* (1343)
▸ Rom 5:21

5:18
1 Cor 15:22
ᵍ*dikaiōsis* (1347)
▸ 1 Cor 15:34

¹⁰For since our friendship with God was ᵇrestored by the death of his Son while we were still his enemies, we will certainly be saved through the life of his Son. ¹¹So now we can rejoice in our wonderful new relationship with God because our Lord Jesus Christ has ᶜmade us friends of God.

The Reign of Grace and Life

¹²When Adam sinned, ᵈsin entered the world. Adam's ᵈsin brought death, so death spread to everyone, for everyone sinned. ¹³Yes, people sinned even before the law was given. But it was not counted as sin because there was not yet any law to break. ¹⁴Still, everyone died—from the time of Adam to the time of Moses—even those who did not disobey an explicit commandment of God, as Adam did. Now Adam is a ᵉsymbol, a representation of Christ, who was yet to come.

¹⁵But there is a great difference between Adam's sin and God's gracious gift. For the sin of this one man, Adam, brought death to many. But even greater is God's wonderful grace and his gift of forgiveness to many through this other man, Jesus Christ. ¹⁶And the result of God's gracious gift is very different from the result of that one man's sin. For Adam's sin led to condemnation, but God's free gift leads to our being made right with God, even though we are guilty of many sins. ¹⁷For the sin of this one man, Adam, caused death to rule over many. But even greater is God's wonderful grace and his gift of ᶠrighteousness, for all who receive it will live in triumph over sin and death through this one man, Jesus Christ.

¹⁸Yes, Adam's one sin brings condemnation for everyone, but Christ's one act of righteousness brings a ᵍright relationship

God's Grace (5:15-17, 20-21)

Rom 12:6
Exod 34:5-7
Ezra 9:8
Ps 84:11
Isa 60:10
Hos 14:1-9
Acts 15:11; 20:24
2 Cor 8:9; 12:9
Eph 1:6-7; 2:5-9
2 Tim 1:9
Titus 2:11; 3:7
Heb 4:16; 13:9
Jas 4:6
1 Pet 5:12

The grace of God is theological bedrock for Paul. He never tries to prove that God is gracious, but he assumes it as a fact when presenting the Good News to the Romans (see 3:24; 4:4-5, 16; 5:2, 15-21; 6:14-15; 11:5-6). Paul rules out any idea that we merit our salvation, because God acts by his grace (4:4-5). Our good works do not give us right standing with God—if they did, God would be obliged to reward us for our efforts, just as a worker earns a wage. Instead, he gives salvation as a gift to those he has chosen (11:5-6). Grace is so important to the Christian experience that Paul can refer simply to our "standing in" grace (cp. 5:2) and to our living under the power of grace (6:14-15). Grace now rules over us in the new age of redemption (5:20-21).

The apostle John makes the same point: "The law was given through Moses, but God's unfailing love [grace] and faithfulness came through Jesus Christ" (John 1:17). Neither John nor Paul meant that God's grace was not active in the OT, because God has always dealt graciously with his people. But the overwhelming power of God's grace is displayed for us in and through Jesus Christ.

5:10 *saved through the life of his Son:* Believers already share in the new life that Christ provided through his resurrection (6:11). Through this vital connection with Christ, believers will also be spared from God's wrath in the last day (see also Col 3:4).

5:12 *Adam* is both the name of the original man, Adam, and a Hebrew word that means "human." Paul emphasizes the solidarity of *Adam* with the human race. • *sin entered the world:* The significance that Paul ascribes to this act, and the parallel that he draws between Adam's sin and Christ's act of obedience on the cross, makes clear that Paul views Adam and his sin in the Garden of Eden as historical fact. • *everyone sinned:* Death is universal because sin is universal. It is not clear when or how everyone sinned, but Paul later attributes the condemnation of all people to the sin of Adam, their representative (5:18). • Jewish tradition

is divided on the relationship between *Adam's sin* and the sin and death of human beings generally. Some texts emphasize a solidarity between Adam and all other people, as in "when Adam sinned a death was decreed against those who were to be born" (*2 Baruch* 23:4). Other texts insist that people die because of their own sin: "Adam is, therefore, not the cause, except only for himself, but each of us had become our own Adam" (*2 Baruch* 54:19).

5:13-14 Paul continues his explanation of "everyone sinned" (5:12) by stating that people who died between the times of Adam and Moses were not subject to specific commandments from God. Therefore, their condemnation was not only because of their own sin. It was because of their union with Adam, who sinned by violating *an explicit commandment of God.*

5:15 Paul uses the word *many* in contrast with *one. Many* does not

always mean *all,* but it can include all people if the context suggests it. Clearly, the many who suffer death because of *Adam* includes everyone (see 5:12), but Paul makes it clear elsewhere that the *many* who receive the *gift of forgiveness* through *Jesus Christ,* sadly, does not include everyone (see 11:1-5).

5:17 Both *Adam* and *Jesus Christ* committed a single act whose influence extends to all the people that they represent. Adam represents all people. People must *receive* the *gift of righteousness* to be represented by Christ.

5:18 *Christ's one act of righteousness* refers to his death on the cross, a righteous act because Christ chose to die in obedience to the Father's will (see John 10:18). • *new life for everyone:* Paul is not teaching that all people will experience the new life that Christ won through his death on the cross. New life is available to everyone through Christ, but not everyone receives it.

with God and new life for everyone. ¹⁹Because one person disobeyed God, many became sinners. But because one other person obeyed God, many will be made righteous.

²⁰God's law was given so that all people could see how sinful they were. But as people sinned more and more, God's wonderful grace became more abundant. ²¹So just as sin ruled over all people and brought them to death, now God's wonderful ʰgrace rules instead, giving us ⁱright standing with God and resulting in eternal life through Jesus Christ our Lord.

Freedom from Bondage to Sin (6:1-23)
"Dead to Sin" through Union with Christ

6 Well then, should we keep on ʲsinning so that God can show us more and more of his wonderful ᵏgrace? ²Of course not! Since we have died to sin, how can we continue to live in it? ³Or have you forgotten that when we were ᵃjoined with Christ Jesus in baptism, we ᵃjoined him in his death? ⁴For we died and were buried with Christ by baptism. And just as Christ was raised from the dead by the glorious power of the Father, now we also may live new lives.

⁵Since we have been united with him in his death, we will also be raised to life as he was. ⁶We know that our old sinful selves were crucified with Christ so that sin might lose its power in our lives. We are no longer slaves to sin. ⁷For when we died with Christ we were set free from the power of sin. ⁸And since we died with Christ, we know we will also live with him. ⁹We are sure of this because Christ was raised from the dead, and he will never die again. Death no longer has any power over him. ¹⁰When he died, he died once to break the power of sin. But now that he lives, he lives for the glory of God. ¹¹So you also should consider yourselves to be dead to the power of sin and alive to God through Christ Jesus.

¹²Do not let sin control the way you live; do not give in to sinful desires. ¹³Do not let any part of your body become an instrument of evil to serve sin. Instead, give yourselves completely to God, for you were dead, but now you have new life. So use your whole body as an instrument to do what is right for the glory of God. ¹⁴Sin is no longer your master, for you no longer live under the requirements of the law. Instead, you live under the freedom of God's grace.

Freed from Sin's Power to Serve Righteousness

¹⁵Well then, since God's grace has set us free from the law, does that mean we can go on sinning? Of course not! ¹⁶Don't you realize that you become the slave of whatever

5:19
Phil 2:8

5:20
Rom 4:15; 7:8
Gal 3:19

5:21
Rom 6:23
ʰ*charis* (5485)
▸ Rom 6:1
ⁱ*dikaiosunē* (1343)
▸ Rom 8:10

6:1
Rom 3:5-8
ʲ*hamartia* (0266)
▸ Rom 7:8
ᵏ*charis* (5485)
▸ Gal 1:15

6:2
Rom 8:13
Col 2:20; 3:3

6:3
Gal 3:27
ᵃ*baptizō* (0907)
▸ 1 Cor 12:13

6:4
Eph 4:22-24
Col 2:12; 3:10

6:5
Phil 3:10-11
Col 2:12; 3:1

6:6
Gal 2:20; 5:24
Col 2:12

6:7
1 Pet 4:1

6:9
Acts 2:24

6:10
Heb 7:27

6:11
Rom 7:4
Col 2:20; 3:3

6:13
Rom 12:1
2 Cor 5:14

. . . .

5:20 Many Jews believed that the giving of the law to Israel reversed or mitigated the negative effects of Adam's sin, but Paul says that God's law magnified and illuminated their sins.

6:1 *Well then:* Because Paul has just proclaimed that God multiplies grace where sin increases (5:20), he knows that people will wonder whether this means that sin does not matter in the Christian life.

6:2 *we have died to sin:* As Paul makes clear in 6:3-10, our new relationship to sin is possible because of our vital connection with the death of Jesus. Just as dying means entrance into an entirely new state of being, our relationship with sin is now different because of Christ's death. To be "dead to sin" does not mean to be entirely insensitive to sin and temptation—believers are still involved in a battle with sin (6:12-14). However, Christians no longer have to live as helpless slaves to sin; they can choose not to sin (6:6, 14, 16-22).

6:3 *Baptism* is the rite of initiation into the Christian faith (see "Baptism" at Acts 2:38, 41, p. 1828). It sometimes symbolizes the entire conversion experience, so Paul refers to baptism as the means through which believers are joined to Christ in his death and resurrection (see also 6:4). However, baptism has no value apart from faith.

6:4 *we died and were buried with Christ:* The believer's power over sin and the ability to lead a new life stem from identification with Christ's death, burial, and resurrection (see 6:5, 8). From God's perspective, Jesus' death to sin (see 6:10) is ours as well. His rising to new life means that we also begin to lead a new life, and in the future our bodies will also be raised.

6:6 *our old sinful selves:* Our "old selves" are not a nature that we possess or just one part of who we are; it reflects who we were in Adam. All human beings were born "in Adam." As heirs of the sin and death that he introduced into the world (5:12), we were slaves to the power of sin. But as people who are now in Christ, we have gone through crucifixion with him (see also Gal 2:20). When he died on the cross, we also died to the dominating power of sin that ruled our former selves.

6:8 *We will also live with him* refers to bodily resurrection with Christ (see 6:5). While believers are already raised with Christ spiritually (Eph 2:5-6; Col 2:13), we will also be raised bodily with him at the time of his coming in glory (2 Cor 4:14; Phil 3:21; 1 Thes 4:17; 2 Tim 2:11).

6:10 *he died once to break the power of sin:* Because we died with Jesus (6:4-5), we have also died to sin (6:2). Jesus was never under sin's power in the way that we are, because he had no sin nature from Adam and he never succumbed to temptation (2 Cor 5:21; Heb 4:15). However, when he became human, he entered the arena where sin holds sway, and he was truly vulnerable to sin.

6:12 *Do not let sin control the way you live:* Or *Do not let sin reign in your body, which is subject to death.*

6:14 *you no longer live under the requirements of the law:* With the Messiah's coming, the era governed by the law of Moses came to an end (see Gal 3:19-25). • *you live under the freedom of God's grace:* God's dealings with his people have always been characterized by grace, but grace dominates the new era in which Christians live in Christ. Cp. John 1:17.

6:15 *set us free from the law:* The law of Moses was the governing power of the old covenant era. Believers now live under the governing power of Christ himself.

6:14
Gal 5:18
6:16
John 8:34
2 Pet 2:19
6:17
2 Tim 1:13
6:18
John 8:32
6:19
ᵇ*hagiasmos* (0038)
▸ Rom 6:22
6:20
ᶜ*doulos* (1401)
▸ 1 Cor 7:22
6:22
John 8:32
1 Cor 7:22
1 Pet 1:9; 2:16
ᵈ*hagiasmos* (0038)
▸ 1 Cor 1:30
6:23
John 3:16-21
Gal 6:8
7:2
1 Cor 7:39
7:3
Luke 16:18

you choose to obey? You can be a slave to sin, which leads to death, or you can choose to obey God, which leads to righteous living. [17]Thank God! Once you were slaves of sin, but now you wholeheartedly obey this teaching we have given you. [18]Now you are free from your slavery to sin, and you have become slaves to righteous living.

[19]Because of the weakness of your human nature, I am using the illustration of slavery to help you understand all this. Previously, you let yourselves be slaves to impurity and lawlessness, which led ever deeper into sin. Now you must give yourselves to be slaves to righteous living so that you will become ᵇholy.

[20]When you were ᶜslaves to sin, you were free from the obligation to do right. [21]And what was the result? You are now ashamed of the things you used to do, things that end in eternal doom. [22]But now you are free from the power of sin and have become slaves of God. Now you do those things that lead to ᵈholiness and result in eternal life. [23]For the wages of sin is death, but the free gift of God is eternal life through Christ Jesus our Lord.

Freedom from Bondage to the Law (7:1-25)
Released from the Law, Joined to Christ

7 Now, dear brothers and sisters—you who are familiar with the law—don't you know that the law applies only while a person is living? [2]For example, when a woman marries, the law binds her to her husband as long as he is alive. But if he dies, the laws of marriage no longer apply to her. [3]So while her husband is alive, she would be committing adultery if she married another man. But if her husband dies, she is free from that

. . . .

The Old Realm and the New (5:12–8:39)

Rom 14:17
Ps 2:1-10; 110:2;
145:13
Dan 2:31-45; 7:1-28
Matt 3:2; 6:10; 7:13;
8:11-12; 12:25-28;
13:44-52; 20:25-28
John 18:36
1 Cor 6:9-11;
15:20-28
Gal 5:16-26
Eph 1:3, 20; 2:6;
5:1-20
Col 1:13-14
Heb 6:4-5; 12:18-29
Rev 11:15; 12:10

Jews in Paul's day perceived a contrast between the "present evil age" and a "glorious age to come." Throughout Rom 5–8, Paul uses these contrasting realms to conceptualize our experience of salvation. The old realm is ruled by death (5:12-21), sin (ch 6), the law (ch 7), and sinful nature (8:1-11). The new realm is characterized by life (ch 5), righteous living (ch 6), grace (ch 6), and the Holy Spirit (ch 8). People's destinies are controlled by the realm to which they belong.

Each realm is headed by a man who represents its constituents. The old realm of sin and death is headed by Adam, the first man, while the new realm of forgiveness and life is headed by Christ. By nature, all human beings are in the old realm of sin and death and are represented by Adam, the first man—whose sin and death control the destiny of all people (5:12, 18-19). Those who put their faith in God through Christ are transferred by faith into the new realm of life. God appointed Jesus Christ as a "second Adam" (see 5:14). By obeying God and fulfilling God's will, Jesus won a decisive victory over the realm of sin that Adam had inaugurated (5:18-19). By receiving God's gift of grace (5:17), people accept Jesus as their head and look forward to eternal life.

Those who are in the new realm are identified with Christ and enjoy the benefits of union with him. They have "died with Christ," they have been "buried with Christ," and their present new life with Christ is an anticipation of the day when they will "live with him" forever (6:3-10).

. . . .

6:16 *righteous living* (Greek *dikaiosunē,* "righteousness"): In the first part of Romans, Paul uses this Greek word in a judicial sense, referring (1) to the activity of God to set people in a right relationship with himself or (2) to the righteous standing that believers enjoy as a result of Christ's work (see, e.g., 1:17; 3:21-22; 4:3, 5). Here, Paul uses the same word as it is often used in the OT, meaning the right behavior that God demands from his people.

6:19 Paul uses the Greek word *sarx* (*human nature,* or *flesh*) to refer to the frailty and proneness to sin that characterizes humans. Paul uses the *illustration of slavery* to show the relationship of the human nature to sin.

6:20 *free from the obligation to do right* (literally *free from righteousness*): Paul means either that unbelievers feel no obligation to obey God or that they are unable to do so. But the freedom that they boast of actually makes them slaves to sin.

6:21 *eternal doom* (literally *death*): Throughout chs 5–8, Paul uses *death* to describe the eternal consequences of sin (5:12, 14, 15, 17, 21; 6:16, 23; 7:5, 9-10, 13, 24; 8:2, 6, 13). The language goes back to God's warning to Adam and Eve (Gen 2:17). This death is not primarily physical death; it denotes separation from the fellowship of God that, if not reversed through faith in Christ, will last forever.

7:1 *brothers and sisters:* Literally *brothers;* also in 7:4. See note on 1:13. • Both Jewish Christians and many of the Gentile Christians were *familiar with the law.* Jews were taught the law of Moses from birth. Many of the Gentiles in the church at Rome had been God-fearers, Gentiles who were interested in Judaism and attended the synagogue regularly. • *the law applies only while a person is living:* Paul may be paraphrasing a rabbinic saying: "If a person is dead, he is free from the Torah and the fulfilling of the commandments" (*Babylonian Shabbat* 30a; *baraita Shabbat* 151).

7:2-3 These verses are not an allegory, in which every element of the story has a theological counterpart. Paul simply cites an illustration to make two basic points: Death can release a person from obligation to the law, and freedom from one relationship can allow a person to establish a new one. Paul applies the illustration in 7:4.

law and does not commit adultery when she remarries.

4So, my dear brothers and sisters, this is the point: You died to the power of the law when you died with Christ. And now you are united with the one who was raised from the dead. As a result, we can produce a harvest of good deeds for God. 5When we were controlled by our old nature, sinful desires were at work within us, and the law aroused these evil desires that produced a harvest of sinful deeds, resulting in death. 6But now we have been released from the law, for we died to it and are no longer captive to its power. Now we can serve God, not in the old way of obeying the letter of the law, but in the new way of living in the Spirit.

The History and Experience of Jews under the Law

7Well then, am I suggesting that the elaw of God is sinful? Of course not! In fact, it was the elaw that showed me my sin. I would never have known that coveting is wrong if the elaw had not said, "You must not covet." 8But fsin used this command to arouse all kinds of covetous desires within me! If there were no law, fsin would not have that power. 9At one time I lived without understanding the law. But when I learned the command not to covet, for instance, the power of sin came to life, 10and I died. So I discovered that the law's commands, which were supposed to bring life, brought spiritual death instead. 11Sin took advantage of those commands and deceived me; it used the commands to kill me. 12But still, the glaw itself is holy, and its commands are holy and right and good.

13But how can that be? Did the law, which is good, cause my death? Of course not! Sin used what was good to bring about my condemnation to death. So we can see how terrible sin really is. It uses God's good commands for its own evil purposes.

14So the trouble is not with the law, for it is spiritual and good. The trouble is with me, for I am all too human, a slave to sin. 15I don't really understand myself, for I want to do what is right, but I don't do it. Instead, I do what I hate. 16But if I know that what I am doing is wrong, this shows that I agree that the law is good. 17So I am not the one doing wrong; it is sin living in me that does it.

18And I know that nothing good lives in me, that is, in my sinful nature. I want to do what is right, but I can't. 19I want to do what is good, but I don't. I don't want to do what is wrong, but I do it anyway. 20But if I

Ref	Cross-references
7:4	Rom 6:6; 8:2
	Gal 5:18
	Col 2:14
	1 Pet 2:24
7:5	Rom 6:21; 8:8
	Gal 5:19-21
7:6	2 Cor 3:6
	Gal 5:22
	Phil 3:3
7:7	*Exod 20:17
	*Deut 5:21
	Rom 4:15
	enomos (3551)
	▸ Rom 7:12
7:8	Rom 4:15
	fhamartia (0266)
	▸ Rom 8:2
7:10	Lev 18:5
	Rom 10:5
	2 Cor 3:7
	Gal 3:12
7:11	Gen 3:13
	Heb 3:13
7:12	1 Tim 1:8
	gnomos (3551)
	▸ Rom 8:2
7:14	1 Kgs 21:20-25
	Rom 3:9; 6:6
7:15	Gal 5:17
7:18	Gen 6:5; 8:21
	John 3:6
	Rom 8:3

. . . .

7:4 Christians have *died to the power of the law* (literally *died to the law*) and so are no longer bound to it. Paul often refers to the law of Moses as representing the old regime of sin and death, but through union with Christ in his death, believers are set free.

7:5 *When we were controlled by our old nature* (literally *When we were in the flesh*): Although "flesh" can refer to the human body in a neutral sense (see 8:3, which speaks of Christ coming "in the flesh"), Paul more often uses the word negatively, to denote human existence apart from God. To be "in the flesh" is to be dominated by sin and its hostility to God. • *the law aroused these evil desires*: The law of God is a good thing in itself (see 7:12), but it arouses sinful tendencies by provoking the rebellion that is in people's hearts. When we are in rebellion against God, his commands spark in us a desire to do the exact opposite of what he commands.

7:6 *the letter of the law* (literally *the letter*): Paul uses the word *letter* to refer to the law, which was engraved on tablets of stone and consisted of individual letters (see 2:29; 2 Cor 3:5-7).

7:7-25 Well then (see note on 6:1): Paul has just said some rather negative things about the law, and he now explains how God's law is good in order to guard against any notion that it is evil in itself.

7:7 *"You must not covet"*: See Exod 20:17; Deut 5:21.

7:8 *sin used this command* (literally *sin took an opportunity through this command*): The word *opportunity* is a military term for a position seized in enemy territory that becomes a base of operations (see 7:11). By expressing God's demands, the commandments stimulate rebellion in sinful human beings. The commandments of God become an occasion for sin to accomplish its deadly purposes. • *sin would not have that power*: The law, by clearly expressing God's will, makes people more accountable than they would be without it. The law of Moses did not solve Israel's sin problem but exposed and exacerbated it. This is always the effect that God's law, by itself, has on sinful human beings.

7:9 *At one time I lived without understanding the law:* Paul might be referring to his early childhood, before he came to understand the full demands of the law. • *But when I learned the command:* Paul's experience with the law as he grew to maturity exemplifies every person's experience with it. With the law, we have greater accountability to God, which brings the *power of sin* to life, and the result is greater judgment (7:10; see 4:15; 5:14, 20).

7:10 *which were supposed to bring life:* The OT promised a blessed and secure life to those who obeyed the law (e.g., Lev 18:5, quoted in Rom 10:5). However, human beings inherit from Adam a strong tendency to sin. Therefore, when God's commands come to us, we do not naturally obey them, but resist and disobey them. Instead of bringing life, the law only confirms and exposes our lost and helpless condition. We need a change of heart that the law cannot provide.

7:11 *Sin . . . deceived me:* The language is reminiscent of Gen 3:13—Paul might be thinking of the Fall.

7:17 *I am not the one doing wrong:* Paul is not evading responsibility for his sin (see also 7:20). Rather, he is saying that because he genuinely wants to do what the law commands, some other factor must be causing him to do just the opposite. That factor is *sin living in me*. Paul experiences a divide between his will and his actions.

7:18 *my sinful nature* (literally *my flesh*; also in 7:25): This phrase could refer to Paul's former state as an unredeemed person or to a part of Paul that remains tied to the world and resists the will of God. See note on 6:19.

7:21
Rom 8:2

7:22
Ps 1:2; 40:8

7:23
Gal 5:17
Jas 4:1
1 Pet 2:11

7:25
1 Cor 15:57

8:2
Gal 2:19; 5:1
ʰnomos (3551)
 ▸ Rom 10:4
ⁱhamartia (0266)
 ▸ Rom 14:23

8:3
2 Cor 5:21
Heb 2:14; 4:15

do what I don't want to do, I am not really the one doing wrong; it is sin living in me that does it.

²¹I have discovered this principle of life—that when I want to do what is right, I inevitably do what is wrong. ²²I love God's law with all my heart. ²³But there is another power within me that is at war with my mind. This power makes me a slave to the sin that is still within me. ²⁴Oh, what a miserable person I am! Who will free me from this life that is dominated by sin and death? ²⁵Thank God! The answer is in Jesus Christ our Lord. So you see how it is: In my mind I

really want to obey God's law, but because of my sinful nature I am a slave to sin.

Assurance of Eternal Life in the Spirit (8:1-30)
The Spirit of Life

8 So now there is no condemnation for those who belong to Christ Jesus. ²And because you belong to him, the ʰpower of the life-giving Spirit has freed you from the ʰpower of ⁱsin that leads to death. ³The law of Moses was unable to save us because of the weakness of our sinful nature. So God did what the law could not do. He sent his

The Limitations of Law (7:1-25)

Rom 2:13-29; 3:19-21, 27-28; 4:13-16; 8:3-4, 7; 9:4, 31-32; 10:3-5
Deut 4:44-45; 5:1-33; 6:17-25
Josh 24:19-27
1 Kgs 2:3
Ezra 7:25-26
Ps 1:1-3; 19:7-14; 78:56-59; 119:36, 79, 88, 144
Isa 24:5; 26:4-8
Jer 31:33-34
Hos 4:6; 8:12
Hab 1:4
Matt 5:17-20; 7:12; 22:36-40
Mark 7:8-9; 12:28-34
Luke 16:16-17
John 1:16-17; 7:19
Acts 13:38-39
Gal 2:16-21; 3:2, 10-13, 17-25; 5:1-4
1 Tim 1:5-11
Heb 7:18-19; 8:7-13; 10:1-18
1 Jn 3:4-6

The law was central to God's old covenant with the people of Israel, and many Jews in Paul's day still saw it as critical to how God's people lived. Therefore, in Romans, Paul frequently deals with questions about the law. The pinnacle of his treatment comes in Rom 7, where Paul powerfully argues that the law of Moses, rather than having a positive effect on people's lives, stimulated sin and brought death (7:5).

Paul wants us to realize that the law is not at fault. God's law is good and holy (7:12), but it is powerless to change the human heart. Whether we conclude that Paul (in 7:14-25) is describing the experience of an unbeliever, a mature believer, or an immature believer, the point remains that human sin cannot be overcome by the law. God's law is given to people who, because of their connection with Adam, are already locked under sin's power. They may want to do what God tells them, but they find that they cannot (7:15-20). Deliverance can come only through a new and radical experience of God's power and grace in Jesus Christ (7:25). Through God's Spirit, Jesus rescues us "from the power of sin that leads to death" (8:2).

If God's good and holy law cannot rescue us from our predicament and save us, how much less helpful are all human laws that people rely on for religious or spiritual well-being. Whether those laws come from a religious figure, a tradition we have inherited, or a church we attend, none of them can change the human soul. They can tell us what to do, but they cannot empower us to do it. God's law can provide guidelines in the new life God has given us by grace, but it can never substitute for the power of God's grace, made available through the work of Christ.

7:21 *principle of life* (literally *law*): Paul is referring to a regular occurrence, such as when we speak of the "law of gravity." The struggle between wanting to *do what is right* and instead doing *what is wrong* reveals a regular pattern operating in the human sphere.

7:22 *with all my heart* (literally *in my inner person*): The Greeks used this phrase to denote the spiritual or immortal side of human beings (cp. 2 Cor 4:16; Eph 3:16).

7:23 *another power. . . . This power* (literally *another law. . . . This law*): Paul plays on the word *law* in these verses. Opposed to God's law (7:22) is another law, a ruling *power* that prevents Paul from submitting to God's law even though he fully agrees with it.

7:24 *this life that is dominated by sin and death* (literally *this body of death*): Sin is so invasive that it affects the

whole person, particularly our interactions in the physical world.

8:1 *So now there is no condemnation:* Paul concludes from the argument of chs 5–7 that neither sin (ch 6) nor the law (ch 7) can keep believers from having eternal life (ch 5). Paul can triumphantly proclaim that *those who belong to Christ Jesus* need not fear that they will be condemned for their sins.

8:2 *you belong . . . freed you:* Some manuscripts read *I belong . . . freed me.* A scribe might have changed an original *you* into *I/me* at some point. • *the power* (literally *the law*) *of the life-giving Spirit:* This reference to *power* or *law* could refer to the law of Moses, which the Spirit can use to produce life. But because Paul does not portray the law as a life-giving entity, "law" here, as in 7:23, probably means *principle* or *power.* The Holy Spirit is a power that frees the believer from *the power*

(literally *the law*) *of sin that leads to death.*

8:3 *our sinful nature:* Literally *our flesh;* similarly in 8:4-9, 12. See note on 6:19. • *in a body like the bodies we sinners have:* Jesus identified with sinful people so that he could be their representative and redeem them. Paul also implies that Jesus' incarnate nature was not exactly like ours; born of a virgin through the power of the Holy Spirit, Jesus did not inherit a sinful nature from Adam. • *a sacrifice for our sins:* In the Greek OT, this phrase frequently describes a sin offering, and three of the eight NT occurrences also have this meaning (Heb 10:6, 8; 13:11). Christ was the sin offering that brought forgiveness and turned away God's wrath. God condemned sin in Christ, our substitute, so that we could escape condemnation.

own Son in a body like the bodies we sinners have. And in that body God declared an end to sin's control over us by giving his Son as a sacrifice for our sins. [4]He did this so that the just requirement of the law would be fully satisfied for us, who no longer follow our [j]sinful nature but instead follow the Spirit.

[5]Those who are dominated by the sinful nature think about sinful things, but those who are controlled by the Holy Spirit think about things that please the Spirit. [6]So letting your sinful nature control your mind leads to death. But letting the Spirit control your mind leads to life and [k]peace. [7]For the sinful nature is always hostile to God. It never did obey God's laws, and it never will. [8]That's why those who are still under the control of their sinful nature can never please God.

[9]But you are not controlled by your sinful nature. You are controlled by the Spirit if you have the Spirit of God living in you. (And remember that those who do not have the Spirit of Christ living in them do not belong to him at all.) [10]And Christ lives within you, so even though your body will die because of sin, the [a]Spirit gives you life because you have been made [b]right with God.

[11]The Spirit of God, who raised Jesus from the dead, lives in you. And just as God raised Christ Jesus from the dead, he will [c]give life to your mortal bodies by this same Spirit living within you.

[12]Therefore, dear brothers and sisters, you have no obligation to do what your sinful nature urges you to do. [13]For if you live by its dictates, you will die. But if through the power of the [d]Spirit you put to death the deeds of your sinful nature, you will live.

The Spirit of Adoption

[14]For all who are led by the Spirit of God are children of God.

[15]So you have not received a spirit that makes you fearful slaves. Instead, you received God's Spirit when he [e]adopted you as his own children. Now we call him, [f]"Abba, Father." [16]For his Spirit joins with our spirit to affirm that we are God's children. [17]And since we are his children, we are his heirs. In fact, together with Christ we are [g]heirs of God's glory. But if we are to share his glory, we must also share his suffering.

The Spirit of Glory

[18]Yet what we suffer now is nothing compared to the glory he will reveal to us later.

8:4
Gal 5:16, 25
[i]*sarx* (4561)
▸ 1 Cor 5:5

8:5
Gal 5:19-23

8:6
Gal 6:8
[k]*eirēnē* (1515)
▸ Rom 14:19

8:9
Gal 4:6

8:10
[a]*pneuma* (4151)
▸ Rom 8:13
[b]*dikaiosunē* (1343)
▸ Rom 10:10

8:11
[c]*zōopoieō* (2227)
▸ 1 Cor 15:22

8:13
Gal 6:8
Col 3:5
[d]*pneuma* (4151)
▸ 1 Cor 5:3

8:14
Gal 3:26

8:15
Gal 4:5-6
[e]*huiothesia* (5206)
▸ Rom 8:23
[f]*abba patēr* (0005, 3962)
▸ Gal 4:6

8:16
2 Cor 1:22

8:17
Gal 3:29; 4:7
[s]*sunklēronomos* (4789)
▸ Eph 3:6

. . . .

8:4 *just requirement of the law . . . fully satisfied for* (Greek *en,* "in") *us:* The Greek preposition *en* might indicate that the law is fulfilled *in* us because of our connection with Jesus Christ, who perfectly fulfilled the law for us. It could also mean that by setting us free from sin's power, Jesus Christ enables us to please God and fulfill the true intention of the law. • As in the OT (see Gen 6:3, 12; Ps 78:39; Isa 40:6), *sinful nature* refers to human weakness and bondage to sin (also in 8:5-9, 12-13). Paul uses the phrase to describe the conflict between the ingrained human tendency to sin and the Holy Spirit.

8:5 *think about sinful things:* This phrase describes the general nature of a person's will, not just the mental process of thought (see also 12:3; 15:5; Phil 2:2, 5).

8:6 *Peace* here does not refer merely to peace of mind; instead, as opposed to *death,* it implies an objective state of peace with God (see note on 5:1).

8:9 *You are controlled by the Spirit:* In contrast to unbelievers, who continue to live under the domination of Adam's *sinful nature,* the Holy Spirit directs the lives of believers. The Spirit does not take away human initiative or make it impossible for believers to sin. However, as the most powerful force in believers' lives, the Spirit makes it possible for

them to resist the continuing power of sin.

8:10 *the Spirit gives you life* (or *your spirit is alive*): The Spirit opposes sin (which leads to physical death) and brings resurrection from the dead.

8:11 *by this same Spirit:* The Holy Spirit is the agent of the resurrection of our *bodies.* Some manuscripts read "*because of* the same Spirit," which would mean that the Spirit is the guarantee that our bodies will be raised (cp. Eph 1:14).

8:12 *brothers and sisters:* Literally *brothers;* also in 8:29. See note on 1:13.

8:13 *deeds of your sinful nature:* Literally *deeds of the body.* • *you will die:* Death is the consequence of sin. Those who consistently yield to sin will suffer spiritual death (eternal condemnation). The presence of the Holy Spirit in the lives of believers makes it possible for them to turn away from sin. The result is eternal life (*you will live*).

8:14 *children* (literally *sons*) *of God:* In the OT, this phrase referred to Israel, the people God called to be his own (see especially Exod 4:22; Jer 3:19; 31:9; Hos 11:1). Paul uses it to remind believers that they enjoy an intimate relationship with God and that they will inherit many of the promises and blessings given to Israel. Christians are no longer

minors or slaves, but mature children with full rights (see Gal 4:1-7).

8:15 *you received God's Spirit when he adopted you as his own children* (literally *you received a spirit of sonship*): According to Greco-Roman customs of adoption, a man had the right to adopt a son and to confer on that child all the legal rights and privileges that would be given to a natural child. This practice extended even to the imperial family. The Roman emperor Julius Caesar adopted Octavian as his heir; Octavian, using the name Augustus, later ruled the Roman empire. Paul's concept of adoption is also rooted in the OT and Judaism (Exod 4:22; Deut 1:31; Hos 11:1; see also Rom 9:4; Gal 4:5; Eph 1:5). • *Abba* is an Aramaic term for "father." This word was used in an intimate family context ("Daddy"). Jesus used this word to address God (Mark 14:36); all those who become children of God through Jesus have the privilege of addressing God in the same way.

8:17 Jesus is heir to all of God's promises (Mark 12:1-12; Gal 3:18-19; Heb 1:2), and as those who belong to Jesus, we *share* with him in that glorious inheritance. However, just as it was for Jesus, our path to *glory* is also marked by *suffering.* We experience the difficulties that come from striving to live righteously in a world dominated by sin (2 Cor 1:5; Phil 1:29; 3:10).

8:18
2 Cor 4:17
1 Pet 1:6-7

8:20
Gen 3:17-19

8:21
Acts 3:21
ʰ*eleutheria* (1657)
▸ 1 Cor 10:29

8:23
ⁱ*huiothesia* (5206)
▸ Rom 9:4
ʲ*apolutrōsis* (0629)
▸ 1 Cor 1:30

8:24
Heb 11:1
ᵏ*elpis* (1680)
▸ 1 Cor 13:13
ᵃ*sōzō* (4982)
▸ Rom 10:9

8:26
John 14:16

8:28
ᵇ*klētos* (2822)
▸ Rom 11:29

8:29
1 Pet 1:2
ᶜ*proginōskō* (4267)
▸ Rom 11:2
ᵈ*proorizō* (4309)
▸ Rom 8:30
ᵉ*prōtotokos* (4416)
▸ Col 1:15

8:30
ⁱ*proorizō* (4309)
▸ 1 Cor 2:7

8:31
Ps 118:6

8:34
1 Jn 2:1

8:35
ᵍ*christos* (5547)
▸ 2 Cor 5:10

8:36
*Ps 44:22

8:37
John 16:33
1 Jn 5:4

¹⁹For all creation is waiting eagerly for that future day when God will reveal who his children really are. ²⁰Against its will, all creation was subjected to God's curse. But with eager hope, ²¹the creation looks forward to the day when it will join God's children in glorious ʰfreedom from death and decay. ²²For we know that all creation has been groaning as in the pains of childbirth right up to the present time. ²³And we believers also groan, even though we have the Holy Spirit within us as a foretaste of future glory, for we long for our bodies to be released from sin and suffering. We, too, wait with eager hope for the day when God will give us our full rights as his ⁱadopted children, including the ʲnew bodies he has promised us. ²⁴We were given this ᵏhope when we were ᵃsaved. (If we already have something, we don't need to ᵏhope for it. ²⁵But if we look forward to something we don't yet have, we must wait patiently and confidently.)

²⁶And the Holy Spirit helps us in our weakness. For example, we don't know what God wants us to pray for. But the Holy Spirit prays for us with groanings that cannot be expressed in words. ²⁷And the Father who knows all hearts knows what the Spirit is saying, for the Spirit pleads for us believers in harmony with God's own will. ²⁸And we know that God causes everything to work together for the good of those who love God and are ᵇcalled according to his purpose

for them. ²⁹For God ᶜknew his people in advance, and he ᵈchose them to become like his Son, so that his Son would be the ᵉfirstborn among many brothers and sisters. ³⁰And having ᶠchosen them, he called them to come to him. And having called them, he gave them right standing with himself. And having given them right standing, he gave them his glory.

Nothing Can Separate Us from God's Love (8:31-39)

³¹What shall we say about such wonderful things as these? If God is for us, who can ever be against us? ³²Since he did not spare even his own Son but gave him up for us all, won't he also give us everything else? ³³Who dares accuse us whom God has chosen for his own? No one—for God himself has given us right standing with himself. ³⁴Who then will condemn us? No one—for Christ Jesus died for us and was raised to life for us, and he is sitting in the place of honor at God's right hand, pleading for us.

³⁵Can anything ever separate us from ᵍChrist's love? Does it mean he no longer loves us if we have trouble or calamity, or are persecuted, or hungry, or destitute, or in danger, or threatened with death? ³⁶(As the Scriptures say, "For your sake we are killed every day; we are being slaughtered like sheep.") ³⁷No, despite all these things, overwhelming victory is ours through Christ, who loved us.

8:19-21 *All creation* includes animals, plants, and the earth itself. Paul follows OT precedent (see especially Ps 65:12-13; Isa 24:4; Jer 4:28; 12:4) by personifying the created world. • *waiting eagerly . . . looks forward:* Just as the entire world was harmed by Adam's fall into sin, it will share in the blessings that God has promised his people.

8:19 *his children:* Literally *his sons.*

8:22 The *pains of childbirth* is a metaphor for the longing of creation (see also Matt 24:8; Mark 13:8; John 16:20-22).

8:23 *we believers also groan:* "Groaning" expresses a frustrated longing for God's deliverance from the difficulties and oppression of this life (see Exod 3:7; Lam 1:22; Ezek 24:17; 2 Cor 5:2). • *we have the Holy Spirit within us as a foretaste of future glory* (literally *we have the first harvest of the Spirit*): In the OT, the phrase *first harvest* or *firstfruits* often describes the offering of the first and best part of a harvest to God (see Exod 23:19; Lev 2:12; 23:10; cp. 1 Cor 15:20, 23). The Holy Spirit is God's pledge that he will see his work

in us through to its conclusion (see Eph 1:14). • *wait with eager hope for the day when God will give us our full rights as his adopted children:* Literally *wait anxiously for sonship.* Although we have already been *adopted* by God as his *children,* the *full rights* of that adoption—our inheritance (see 8:17)—are not yet ours. In this life, Christians live in tension between the "already" of redemption and the "not yet" of the glory to be revealed.

8:24 *we don't need to hope for it:* Some manuscripts read *we don't need to wait for it.*

8:26 *groanings that cannot be expressed in words:* This might refer to speech that does not take the form of human language, such as when believers, uncertain of what to pray, utter meaningless sounds in prayer. The groanings in question are the Spirit's, not ours. When we do not know how to pray, the Spirit is interceding for us before God.

8:27 *for us believers:* Literally *for God's holy people.*

8:28 *And we know that God causes*

everything to work together: Some manuscripts read *And we know that everything works together.*

8:29 *would be the firstborn:* Or *would be supreme.*

8:30 *gave them his glory:* Elsewhere in this passage, the *glory* Christians will experience is consistently in the future (8:18, 21, 23). The past tense here refers to God's past decision to glorify us in the future. We have not yet entered into our inheritance, but the Father has irrevocably determined to give us his glory.

8:31 *such wonderful things:* Paul is referring to everything he has taught in chs 5–8 about the blessings and sense of assurance that believers receive from their relationship with God.

8:32 *did not spare even his own Son:* Behind this language is the story about Abraham's willingness to offer his only son, Isaac (Gen 22:12, 16). Isaac, however, was not actually sacrificed. God's not sparing his only Son went the full course: He handed him over to the shameful and painful death of crucifixion.

8:36 This quotation is from Ps 44:22.

38And I am convinced that nothing can ever separate us from God's love. Neither death nor life, neither angels nor demons, neither our fears for today nor our worries about tomorrow—not even the powers of hell can separate us from God's love. 39No power in the sky above or in the earth below—indeed, nothing in all creation will ever be able to separate us from the hlove of God that is revealed in Christ Jesus our Lord.

4. THE DEFENSE OF THE GOSPEL: THE PROBLEM OF ISRAEL (9:1–11:36)

Introduction: The Tension between God's Promises and Israel's Plight (9:1-5)

9 With Christ as my witness, I speak with utter truthfulness. My conscience and the Holy Spirit confirm it. 2My heart is filled with bitter sorrow and unending grief 3for my people, my Jewish brothers and sisters. I would be willing to be forever cursed—cut off from Christ!—if that would save them. 4They are the people of Israel, chosen to be God's iadopted children. God revealed his glory to them. He made covenants with them and gave them his law. He gave them the privilege of worshiping him and receiving his wonderful promises. 5Abraham,

Isaac, and Jacob are their ancestors, and Christ himself was an Israelite as far as his human nature is concerned. And he is God, the one who rules over everything and is worthy of eternal praise! Amen.

Defining the Promise (Part 1): God's Sovereign Election (9:6-29)

The Israel within Israel

6Well then, has God failed to fulfill his promise to Israel? No, for not all who are born into the nation of Israel are truly members of God's people! 7Being descendants of Abraham doesn't make them truly Abraham's children. For the Scriptures say, "Isaac is the son through whom your descendants will be counted," though Abraham had other children, too. 8This means that Abraham's physical descendants are not necessarily children of God. Only the children of the promise are considered to be Abraham's children. 9For God had promised, "I will return about this time next year, and Sarah will have a son."

10This son was our ancestor Isaac. When he married Rebekah, she gave birth to twins. 11But before they were born, before they had done anything good or bad, she received a message from God. (This message shows that God chooses people according

8:38
John 10:28
Col 3:3

8:39
Rom 5:3-8
hagapē (0026)
▸ Rom 13:10

9:1
1 Tim 2:7

9:2-3
Exod 32:32
Rom 10:1

9:4
Exod 4:22
Deut 4:13; 7:6
Eph 2:12
ihuiothesia (5206)
▸ Gal 4:5

9:5
John 1:1, 18
Rom 1:3
Titus 2:13
2 Pet 1:1
1 Jn 5:20

9:6
Num 23:19
Rom 2:28
Gal 6:16

9:7
*Gen 21:12
Heb 11:18

9:8
Rom 8:14
Gal 3:16; 4:23

9:9
*Gen 18:10, 14

9:10
Gen 25:21

8:38 *nor demons:* Literally *nor rulers.*

9:1–11:36 In this section, Paul takes up the problem raised by the unbelief of so many Jews. If God had promised salvation to Israel yet so few Jews were being saved, how could Jesus truly be the fulfillment of God's plan (9:1-5)? In his response to this objection, Paul cites the OT as evidence that God had always intended to save only a remnant of Israel (9:6-29), and he faults the Jews for refusing to embrace Christ (9:30–10:21). Paul then shows that God has not discarded Israel from his plan of salvation. Many Jews have already believed in Christ (11:1-10), and many more will believe in the future (11:12-26).

9:2-3 Paul does not explicitly say why he has such *bitter sorrow* for his *Jewish brothers and sisters.* Yet his willingness to become *cursed* on their behalf *if that would save them* makes clear that the failure of most Jews to respond to Jesus and be saved stimulated his agony (see also 10:1).

9:3 *my Jewish brothers and sisters:* Literally *my brothers.* Cp. note on 1:13. • *I would be willing to be forever cursed* (Greek *anathema*): Anathema is used in the Greek OT to translate a Hebrew expression that means "set apart for God," which usually has the negative sense of something destined to be destroyed as an offering to God (see Lev 27:28-29;

Josh 6:17-18; 7:1, 11-13; 22:20; 1 Sam 15:3; 1 Chr 2:7). Paul knows that he cannot, in fact, be *cut off from Christ.* Paul is echoing the offer of Moses, who pled with God to kill him but to spare the people (Exod 32:30-32).

9:4 Up to this point in Romans, Paul has called the Jewish people *Jews.* His shift to *people of Israel,* here and throughout most of chs 9–11, is significant. *Jew* connotes national identity, but *Israel* emphasizes the covenant relationship of the people with God. • *chosen to be God's adopted children* (literally *chosen for sonship*): The OT called Israel God's *son* or *child* to emphasize that God had selected Israel to be his own people (e.g., Exod 4:22; Jer 3:19; 31:9; Hos 11:1). Israel's adopted status meant that they received God's blessing and promises, not that they were necessarily saved. • *covenants:* The OT includes several covenants between God and the people of Israel: one with Abraham (Gen 17), one with the nation through Moses at Mount Sinai (Exod 19–24), and one with David (2 Sam 7:8-16; 23:5). See also "God's Covenant Relationships" at Gen 12:1-9, p. 44.

9:5 *Christ* came from the people of Israel, and God first made his promises of salvation to them. • *And he is God, the one who rules over everything and is worthy of eternal praise! Amen.* Or *May*

God, the one who rules over everything, be praised forever. Amen.

9:6 *are truly members of God's people* (literally *are Israel*): "Israel" can refer to the people of Israel in a biological sense, i.e., everyone descended from Jacob. But in the latter part of the OT and in Judaism, the idea of a "righteous remnant" within Israel developed (see "The Remnant" at Isa 11:10-16, p. 1126). On at least one occasion in the NT, Israel refers to everyone, Jew and Gentile, who belongs to God in a spiritual sense (Gal 6:16). Paul is stating that there is now an "Israel within Israel," a community consisting of both Jews and Gentiles who truly believe (cp. 11:16-17; Gal 6:16).

9:7 This quotation is from Gen 21:12, which God spoke to Abraham when he was reluctant to follow Sarah's advice to banish his son Ishmael, who was born to the slave woman Hagar. God assured Abraham that Sarah's child, Isaac, was the son through whom God's promises would be fulfilled.

9:9 This quotation is from Gen 18:10, 14.

9:10-11 *she gave birth to twins:* Literally *she conceived children through this one man.* No human circumstances differentiated Isaac's sons, Jacob and Esau. Not only were they born to the same mother, but they were also conto his own purposes; 12he calls people, but not according to their good or bad works.) She was told, "Your older son will serve your younger son." 13In the words of the Scriptures, "I loved Jacob, but I rejected Esau."

Objections Answered: The Freedom and Purpose of God

14Are we saying, then, that God was unfair? Of course not! 15For God said to Moses,

"I will show mercy to anyone I choose,
and I will show compassion to anyone I choose."

16So it is God who decides to show mercy. We can neither choose it nor work for it. 17For the Scriptures say that God told Pharaoh, "I have appointed you for the very purpose of displaying my power in you and to spread my fame throughout the earth." 18So you see, God chooses to show mercy to some, and he chooses to harden the hearts of others so they refuse to listen.

19Well then, you might say, "Why does God blame people for not responding? Haven't they simply done what he makes them do?"

20No, don't say that. Who are you, a mere human being, to argue with God? Should the thing that was created say to the one who created it, "Why have you made me like this?" 21When a potter makes jars out of clay, doesn't he have a right to use the same lump of clay to make one jar for decoration and another to throw garbage into? 22In the same way, even though God has the right to show his anger and his power, he is very patient with those on whom his anger falls, who are destined for destruction. 23He does this to make the riches of his glory shine even brighter on those to whom he shows mercy, who were prepared in advance for glory.

God's Calling of a New People: Israel and the Gentiles

24And we are among those whom he selected, both from the Jews and from the Gentiles.

25Concerning the Gentiles, God says in the prophecy of Hosea,

· ·

God Is in Charge (9:5-24)

We human beings always want to think that we are in charge. We think that we are the "captains of our souls"[1] and that by our decisions and actions we can determine what will happen. However, Scripture confronts us with quite a different scenario. Although human decisions and actions are significant, the will of God is vastly more important.

In Rom 9, Paul shows that God determines the course of salvation. Paul constantly explains the unexpected development of salvation history by appealing to what God has said and done. Human decisions alone cannot explain the situation, and God has said that he will show mercy to anyone he chooses (9:15). While theologians will continue to debate the role of God's action and the role of human decision in salvation, God's sovereignty stands out clearly.

The contemporary world has set God to the side and ignores the divine influence on the course of human affairs. But God's decisions really do direct the world as well as the personal histories of those who trust him. We can confidently affirm that "God causes everything to work together for the good of those who love God and are called according to his purpose for them" (8:28).

[1] "Invictus" by W. E. Henley (1849–1903).

· ·

ceived at the same time. Instead, Paul argues, the difference between them was of God's choosing.

9:12 "Your older son will serve your younger son": God spoke these words (Gen 25:23) to Rebekah before the twins were born. As the older of the twins, Esau was Isaac's natural heir. But Esau sold his birthright to Jacob and ceded his position to his brother in fulfillment of God's promise.

9:13 "I loved Jacob, but I rejected (literally *hated*) *Esau":* Paul quotes Mal 1:2-3, where *Jacob*, whose other name is Israel (Gen 32:28), stands for the nation of Israel, and *Esau* stands for Edom. Here, Paul is referring to them as individuals. Just as love can sometimes express a choice, so hate can express rejection. The story of Jacob and Esau illustrates how the sovereign God chooses his own people.

9:14-16 God's choice is not unfair because he owes nothing to his sinful creatures (see note on 4:4-5).

9:15 This quotation from Exod 33:19 focuses on God's nature: God is free from obligation or constraint in bestowing mercy on people.

9:17 *God told Pharaoh:* Paul quotes Exod 9:16 (Greek version). At God's direction, Moses had asked Pharaoh to let the people of Israel leave Egypt for their own land. When Pharaoh stubbornly refused, God displayed miracle after miracle to convince Israel, Pharaoh, and the Egyptians of God's power and authority (see Exod 6:7; 7:5; 9:14-16; 14:31).

9:18 *he chooses to harden the hearts of others so they refuse to listen:* Pharaoh refused to let Israel go because his heart was hardened. God hardened Pharaoh's heart (Exod 9:12), and Pharaoh hardened his own heart (Exod 8:15).

9:20-21 See Isa 29:16; 45:9-10.

9:24-26 God was free to select people *from the Jews* who would have a true spiritual relationship with him; similarly, he was also free to choose some *from the Gentiles* to be saved as well. Paul uses *the prophecy of Hosea* to

"Those who were not my people,
      I will now call my people.
And I will love those
      whom I did not love before."

26And,

"Then, at the place where they were told,
      'You are not my people,'
there they will be called
      'children of the living God.'"

27And concerning Israel, Isaiah the prophet cried out,

"Though the people of Israel are as
      numerous as the sand of the
      seashore,
only a remnant will be saved.
28 For the Lord will carry out his sentence
      upon the earth
quickly and with finality."

29And Isaiah said the same thing in another place:

"If the Lord of Heaven's Armies
      had not spared a few of our children,
we would have been wiped out like Sodom,
      destroyed like Gomorrah."

Understanding Israel's Plight: Christ as the Climax of Salvation History (9:30–10:21)
Israel, the Gentiles, and the Righteousness of God

30What does all this mean? Even though the Gentiles were not trying to follow God's standards, they were made right with God. And it was by faith that this took place. 31But the people of Israel, who tried so hard to get right with God by keeping the law, never succeeded. 32Why not? Because they were trying to get right with God by keeping the law instead of by trusting in him. They jstumbled over the great rock in their path. 33God warned them of this in the Scriptures when he said,

"I am placing a stone in Jerusalem that
      makes people kstumble,
a rock that makes them fall.
But anyone who trusts in him
      will never be disgraced."

10 Dear brothers and sisters, the longing of my heart and my prayer to God is for the people of Israel to be saved. 2I know what enthusiasm they have for God, but it is misdirected zeal. 3For they don't understand God's way of making people right with himself. Refusing to accept God's way, they cling to their own way of getting right with God by trying to keep the law. 4For Christ has already accomplished the purpose for which the alaw was given. As a result, all who believe in him are made right with God.

5For Moses writes that the law's way of making a person right with God requires obedience to all of its commands. 6But faith's

9:26 *Hos 1:10
9:27-28 *Isa 10:22-23; 28:22 *Hos 1:10
9:29 *Isa 1:9
9:30 Gal 2:16 Heb 11:7
9:31 Isa 51:1 Rom 10:2-3 Gal 5:4
9:32 Isa 8:14 jproskomma (4348) ▸Rom 9:33
9:33 *Isa 28:16 Rom 10:11 1 Pet 2:6, 8 kproskomma (4348) ▸Rom 14:13
10:2 Acts 22:3 Gal 1:14
10:3 Rom 9:31-32
10:4 Gal 3:24 anomos (3551) ▸1 Cor 14:21
10:5 Lev 18:5 Ezek 20:11, 13, 21 Rom 7:10

. . . .

reinforce his point. Hosea predicted that God would renew his mercy to the ten northern tribes that had rebelled against God and were under his judgment. Paul saw a principle that applies to Gentiles as well. • *Those who were not my people:* see note on 10:19.

9:25 This quotation is from Hos 2:23.

9:26 *children of the living God:* Literally *sons of the living God.* Hos 1:10.

9:27-28 This quotation is from Isa 10:22-23 (Greek version). • *only a remnant will be saved:* So many Israelites had turned from God that the OT prophets spoke of a true spiritual Israel within the larger nation of Israel (see "The Remnant" at Isa 11:10-16, p. 1126). The remnant would receive salvation, while the rest of the Israelites would suffer condemnation.

9:29 This quotation is from Isa 1:9. • The destruction of the cities of *Sodom* and *Gomorrah* (Gen 19) is a poignant illustration of the reality and severity of God's judgment.

9:31 *who tried so hard to get right with God by keeping the law* (literally *who pursued the law of righteousness*): *Law of righteousness* is an idiom that means

"righteousness through the law."

9:32-33 *by keeping the law:* Literally *by works.* • *The great rock in their path* is Christ. People either build on him by putting their faith in him, or they *stumble* over his message that faith, and not human works, is the key to getting *right with God.*

9:33 This quotation is from Isa 8:14; 28:16 (Greek version). These two texts, along with Ps 118:22, are also quoted together in 1 Pet 2:6-8. The early church likely had a collection of messianic "stone" quotations from the OT that they used to illuminate the significance of Christ (see also Matt 21:42). • *Jerusalem:* Greek *Zion.*

10:1 *Dear brothers and sisters:* Literally *Brothers.* See note on 1:13.

10:2 *Zeal* denotes a passionate and commendable commitment to God and his purposes (see Num 25:6-13). But in Paul's day Jewish zeal was *misdirected* because it failed to understand that Jesus Christ is the pinnacle of God's plan. (For Paul's own misdirected zeal before his conversion to Christ, see Acts 9:1-2; Gal 1:13-14.)

10:3 *God's way of making people right with himself:* See 1:17; 3:21-26. Paul uses this phrase to explain Israel's failure in terms basic to the gospel. God manifested his righteousness through the ministry of Christ, but most Jews did not *understand* it, partly because they were so focused on the law as a way of securing their own righteousness.

10:4 *For Christ has already accomplished the purpose for which the law was given* (or *For Christ is the end of the law,* or *For Christ is the culmination of the law*): The function of the law was to point forward and prepare the way for the Messiah; Jesus' coming does not destroy the law but fulfills all of its requirements, so that the primary requirement for God's people is to *believe in him* (see 3:31; Matt 5:17-18).

10:5 *requires obedience to all of its commands:* See Lev 18:5, where these words encouraged the Israelites to obey the law in order to enjoy long life and prosperity in the land that God was giving them (see also Lev 26:3-13; Deut 28:1-14). Paul sees the implication that if people want to be right with God through the law, they can only do so by obeying all of it.

10:6-8
*Deut 30:12-14

10:9
Matt 10:32
bkardia (2588)
 › 2 Cor 5:12
csōzō (4982)
 › 1 Cor 15:2

10:10
ddikaiosunē (1343)
 › Eph 5:9

10:11
*Isa 28:16
Rom 9:33

10:12
Acts 15:9
Eph 2:4-7

10:13
*Joel 2:32
Acts 2:21

10:15
*Isa 52:7
*Nah 1:15

10:16
*Isa 53:1
John 12:38
Heb 4:2

10:17
Gal 3:2, 5
Col 3:16
epistis (4102)
 › Rom 14:1

10:18
*Ps 19:4

10:19
*Deut 32:21

10:20
*Isa 65:1
Rom 9:30

10:21
*Isa 65:2
Matt 23:37

11:1
Phil 3:5

11:2
1 Sam 12:22
fproginōskō (4267)
 › Gal 3:8

way of getting right with God says, "Don't say in your heart, 'Who will go up to heaven?' (to bring Christ down to earth). 7And don't say, 'Who will go down to the place of the dead?' (to bring Christ back to life again)." 8In fact, it says,

"The message is very close at hand;
   it is on your lips and in your heart."

And that message is the very message about faith that we preach: 9If you confess with your mouth that Jesus is Lord and believe in your bheart that God raised him from the dead, you will be csaved. 10For it is by believing in your heart that you are made dright with God, and it is by confessing with your mouth that you are saved. 11As the Scriptures tell us, "Anyone who trusts in him will never be disgraced." 12Jew and Gentile are the same in this respect. They have the same Lord, who gives generously to all who call on him. 13For "Everyone who calls on the name of the LORD will be saved."

Israel's Accountability

14But how can they call on him to save them unless they believe in him? And how can they believe in him if they have never heard about him? And how can they hear about him unless someone tells them? 15And how will anyone go and tell them without being sent? That is why the Scriptures say, "How beautiful are the feet of messengers who bring good news!"

16But not everyone welcomes the Good News, for Isaiah the prophet said, "LORD, who has believed our message?" 17So efaith

comes from hearing, that is, hearing the Good News about Christ. 18But I ask, have the people of Israel actually heard the message? Yes, they have:

"The message has gone throughout the earth,
   and the words to all the world."

19But I ask, did the people of Israel really understand? Yes, they did, for even in the time of Moses, God said,

"I will rouse your jealousy through
      people who are not even a nation.
   I will provoke your anger through the
      foolish Gentiles."

20And later Isaiah spoke boldly for God, saying,

"I was found by people who were not
      looking for me.
   I showed myself to those who were
      not asking for me."

21But regarding Israel, God said,

"All day long I opened my arms to them,
   but they were disobedient and
      rebellious."

Summary: Israel, the "Elect," and the "Hardened" (11:1-10)

11 I ask, then, has God rejected his own people, the nation of Israel? Of course not! I myself am an Israelite, a descendant of Abraham and a member of the tribe of Benjamin. 2No, God has not rejected his own people, whom he fchose from the very beginning.

10:6-8 Here Paul quotes three phrases from Deut 30:12-14 dealing with the law, and he applies them to the Good News about Christ. We do not need to *go up to heaven* to find Christ (and thus to be made right with God), because God has already brought him *down to earth* as a man. Nor do we need to *go down to the place of the dead* to find Christ, because God has already raised him from the dead. To find Christ, we must simply believe in *the message* that is *close at hand*.

10:11 See Isa 28:16 (Greek version).

10:12 *and Gentile:* Literally *and Greek.*

10:13 Paul quotes Joel 2:32, where *the LORD* in Hebrew is *Yahweh*, the personal *name* of God (see Exod 3:15). However, as 10:12 makes clear, *the Lord* in Romans is Jesus Christ. This verse shows that Christians from the time of the apostles have associated Jesus with God.

10:14 It is natural to presume that the pronoun *they* refers to "all who call on

him" from 10:12 or "everyone" from 10:13. While this verse probably does refer to all people, it also continues the accusation against Israel from 10:2-3 (see 10:18). Paul argues that Israel was in a position to know what God was doing through Jesus Christ, so they were culpable for their failure to understand or accept it. Israel was guilty both of failing to understand God's plan in light of Christ (10:3-4) and of focusing so much attention on the law that they missed Christ when he arrived (9:30-32).

10:15 This quotation is from Isa 52:7.

10:16 This quotation is from Isa 53:1.

10:18 *Yes, they have:* Paul quotes Ps 19:4 to show that the *message* of Good News was universally available through creation. And by the time Paul wrote Romans, early Christian missionaries had spread the Good News through most of the Roman empire. Most Jews would have had ample opportunity to hear the message.

10:19 *rouse your jealousy . . . provoke your anger:* This quotation from Deut 32:21 concerns God's punishment of Israel for their idolatry. In Paul's day, Israel remained guilty of idolatry because it put the law in place of God himself. God's punishment involved using the Gentiles, *people who are not even a nation*, to make Israel jealous and angry (11:12-32 elaborates on this theme).

10:20 This quotation is from Isa 65:1 (Greek version). In Isaiah, the words *people who were not looking for me* refer to the people of Israel. As in 9:25-26, Paul applies them to the Gentiles to show that God has opened the way for them to be a part of the people of God.

10:21 This quotation is from Isa 65:2 (Greek version).

11:2 *chose from the very beginning:* Before the people of Israel could do anything to earn their status, God selected them to be his people based

Do you realize what the Scriptures say about this? Elijah the prophet complained to God about the people of Israel and said, ³"LORD, they have killed your prophets and torn down your altars. I am the only one left, and now they are trying to kill me, too."

⁴And do you remember God's reply? He said, "No, I have 7,000 others who have never bowed down to Baal!"

⁵It is the same today, for a few of the people of Israel have remained faithful because of God's grace—his undeserved kindness in choosing them. ⁶And since it is through God's kindness, then it is not by their good works. For in that case, God's grace would not be what it really is—free and undeserved.

⁷So this is the situation: Most of the people of Israel have not found the favor of God they are looking for so earnestly. A few have—the ones God has chosen—but the hearts of the rest were hardened. ⁸As the Scriptures say,

"God has put them into a deep sleep.
To this day he has shut their eyes so they do not see,
and closed their ears so they do not hear."

⁹Likewise, David said,

"Let their bountiful table become a snare,
a trap that makes them think all is well.

Let their blessings cause them to stumble,
and let them get what they deserve.
¹⁰ Let their eyes go blind so they cannot see,
and let their backs be bent forever."

Defining the Promise (Part 2): The Future of Israel (11:11-32)

God's Purpose in Israel's Rejection

¹¹Did God's people stumble and fall beyond recovery? Of course not! They were disobedient, so God made salvation available to the Gentiles. But he wanted his own people to become jealous and claim it for themselves. ¹²Now if the Gentiles were enriched because the people of Israel turned down God's offer of salvation, think how much greater a blessing the world will share when they finally accept it.

¹³I am saying all this especially for you Gentiles. God has appointed me as the apostle to the Gentiles. I stress this, ¹⁴for I want somehow to make the people of Israel jealous of what you Gentiles have, so I might save some of them. ¹⁵For since their rejection meant that God ᵍoffered salvation to the rest of the world, their acceptance will be even more wonderful. It will be life for those who were dead!

The Interrelationship of Jews and Gentiles: Warning to Gentiles

¹⁶And since Abraham and the other patriarchs were holy, their descendants will also

11:3
*1 Kgs 19:10, 14

11:4
*1 Kgs 19:18

11:5
Rom 9:27

11:6
Rom 4:4

11:7
Rom 9:31

11:8
*Deut 29:4
*Isa 29:10
Matt 13:14
John 12:40
Acts 28:26-27

11:9-10
*Ps 69:22-23

11:11
Acts 13:46; 18:6

11:14
1 Cor 9:20
2 Tim 1:9

11:15
Luke 15:24, 32
Rom 5:10
ᵍ*katallagē* (2643)
▸ 1 Cor 7:11

---

on his grace alone. • *Elijah the prophet:* In 1 Kgs 19:1-18, the apostate King Ahab had slaughtered many of the Lord's prophets, and Ahab's wife Jezebel threatened Elijah with the same fate. Elijah fled to the wilderness, where he bemoaned his fate. God responded with the assurance that many faithful people remained. Paul found the present situation to be somewhat parallel. While many Jews did not believe, and some were even hostile, God was (and is) still working to preserve a believing remnant.

11:3 This quotation is from 1 Kgs 19:10, 14.

11:4 This quotation is from 1 Kgs 19:18.

11:5 *for a few of the people of Israel* (literally *for a remnant*): Paul returns to the OT concept of the remnant that he used in 9:27-29. This solid core of godly Israelites represents God's pledge of his continuing faithfulness to his promises and to his people.

11:7-8 *the hearts of the rest were hardened:* This is God's own work; God has *put them into a deep sleep* and *shut*

their eyes. See Acts 13:46-48; 18:6.

11:8 This quotation is from Isa 29:10; Deut 29:4.

11:9-10 This quotation is from Ps 69:22-23 (Greek version).

11:11 *so God made salvation available to the Gentiles:* The offer of salvation to the Gentiles is the purpose, not just the result, of Israel's disobedience. Paul emphasizes that God had the salvation of Gentiles in view all along, and, ultimately, the salvation of many Jews as well. • *he wanted his own people to become jealous:* The theme of jealousy comes from Deut 32:21, which Paul quoted in 10:19. The sight of Gentiles enjoying the blessings of salvation that God had promised to Israel would spur Jews to desire salvation so they could participate in those blessings as well.

11:13-14 *you Gentiles:* Paul addresses the Gentile Christians in Rome with the practical goal of rebuking them for thinking too highly of themselves (11:20), especially in relation to their Jewish brothers and sisters. He shows that their enjoyment of salvation de-

pends entirely on God's kindness (11:22), and that God's final goal is to stimulate repentance among the Jews (11:23). • *I stress this:* Paul devoted himself to the conversion of Gentiles because he knew that their salvation would ultimately lead to salvation for Jews as well.

11:15 The context emphasizes God's role in hardening many Jews (11:7-10), so the phrase *their rejection* likely means God's rejection of the unbelieving Jews. • *their acceptance* then refers to God's acceptance of Jews into his Kingdom (see also 14:3 and 15:7). • While the phrase *life for those who were dead* could refer to the new spiritual life that comes to the Jews as a result of their conversion to Christ (see 6:13), the language more naturally suggests the physical resurrection from the dead that occurs when Christ returns in glory (see, e.g., 1 Thes 4:13-18).

11:16 *the entire batch of dough is holy because the portion given as an offering is holy:* This imagery comes from Num 15:17-21, where God commanded the Israelites to take part of their first batch of dough and set it aside as a gift. God's

11:17
Jer 11:16
Eph 2:11-16

11:18
John 4:22

11:20
Rom 12:16

11:22
John 15:2, 14
Heb 3:14

11:23
2 Cor 3:14-16

be holy—just as the entire batch of dough is holy because the portion given as an offering is holy. For if the roots of the tree are holy, the branches will be, too.

¹⁷But some of these branches from Abraham's tree—some of the people of Israel—have been broken off. And you Gentiles, who were branches from a wild olive tree, have been grafted in. So now you also receive the blessing God has promised Abraham and his children, sharing in the rich nourishment from the root of God's special olive tree. ¹⁸But you must not brag about being grafted in to replace the branches that were broken off. You are just a branch, not the root.

¹⁹"Well," you may say, "those branches

were broken off to make room for me." ²⁰Yes, but remember—those branches were broken off because they didn't believe in Christ, and you are there because you do believe. So don't think highly of yourself, but fear what could happen. ²¹For if God did not spare the original branches, he won't spare you either.

²²Notice how God is both kind and severe. He is severe toward those who disobeyed, but kind to you if you continue to trust in his kindness. But if you stop trusting, you also will be cut off. ²³And if the people of Israel turn from their unbelief, they will be grafted in again, for God has the power to graft them back into the tree. ²⁴You, by nature, were a branch cut from a wild olive

. . . .

Jews and Gentiles (11:11-36)

Rom 1:5-6, 16-17;
2:9-10, 24-27; 3:9,
29-30; 9:25-33;
10:11-13; 15:7-13,
27

Deut 7:7-8; 32:19-21
Isa 9:1-3; 49:6
Matt 4:15-16; 8:10-
12; 15:21-28
Luke 21:20-24
Acts 2:38-39;
10:45-46; 11:12-18;
13:42-49; 18:4-6;
26:15-18; 28:23-28
1 Cor 12:13
Gal 2:8-21; 3:8-9,
26-29
Eph 2:11-22; 3:6
Col 3:11

One of the key themes of Romans is that God has incorporated Gentiles into the people of God while remaining faithful to his promises to Israel. In 11:11-32, Paul describes God's plan to save all nations in four distinct stages:

1. *The Good News is proclaimed to the Jews, who respond (mostly) with unbelief.* In the central metaphor of the olive tree, "some of these branches from Abraham's tree . . . have been broken off" (11:17). This stage was already a matter of history and personal experience for Paul—although he shared the Good News with Jews in synagogues all over the eastern Mediterranean basin, many Jews rejected the message (see Acts 13:42-49; 18:4-6; 28:23-28).

2. *Many Gentiles respond to the message with faith.* As the natural branches were broken off, "branches from a wild olive tree have been grafted in" (11:17). After being resisted in the synagogue, Paul and the other apostles offered salvation to the Gentiles, and many responded affirmatively (see Acts 13:48-49; 26:15-18). By the time Paul wrote Romans, the church in Rome was largely a Gentile community.

3. *Many Jews respond to the Good News with faith.* In the future, the natural branches will be "grafted in again" (11:23). As Gentiles enjoy the blessings of salvation, Jews become jealous and respond to the Good News.

4. *God pours out great blessing on the world, including the resurrection from the dead.* When Jews finally turn to the Lord in greater numbers, there will be a "much greater blessing" (11:12), and the dead will be resurrected (11:15). The end of history will see a great community of both Jews and Gentiles praising God for his mercy. Then all people will see and understand the great wisdom and love of God (11:33-36).

. . . .

promises to and blessings on Abraham, Isaac, and Jacob were like a down payment, guaranteeing the completion of God's work among his people.

11:17-24 In Paul's extended metaphor, *God's special olive tree* refers to the people of God. The image is a natural one, because the olive tree is the most widely cultivated fruit tree in the Mediterranean basin, and it was already used as a symbol of Israel in the OT (Jer 11:16; Hos 14:5-6). Paul refers to the Gentile Christians as *branches from a wild olive tree* because they were not originally included among the people of God.

11:18 *You are just a branch, not the root:* By the time Paul wrote to the church in Rome, it was composed

mainly of Gentiles, a common situation in the early Christian communities. This dominant role led many Gentile Christians to brag about their status, while treating Jews and their religious heritage with disdain. Paul reminds the Gentile believers that they enjoy God's blessings only because they have been included in the one people of God, who are rooted in God's promises to Israel.

11:20 *fear what could happen:* In Scripture, fear often means a reverential awe of God that includes the recognition that we must one day stand before him in judgment (see 2 Cor 5:11; 7:1, 11, 15; Phil 2:12; Col 3:22).

11:21 *he won't:* Some manuscripts read *perhaps he won't.*

11:22 *if you stop trusting, you also will be cut off:* Scripture consistently emphasizes that only believers who persevere to the end will be saved. However, Paul's warning leads to debate over the theological implications of his statement. Some think that it implies that genuine believers can stop believing and therefore not be saved in the end. Others argue that we should not press the metaphor so far and that Paul is referring to people who appear to be believers but whose lack of real faith ultimately reveals itself.

11:24 *by nature . . . contrary to nature:* The usual method of enhancing the yield of olive trees involved grafting a shoot from a *cultivated tree* onto a wild olive tree to benefit from the wild tree's

tree. So if God was willing to do something contrary to nature by grafting you into his cultivated tree, he will be far more eager to graft the original branches back into the tree where they belong.

The Salvation of "All Israel"

25I want you to understand this mystery, dear brothers and sisters, so that you will not feel proud about yourselves. Some of the people of Israel have hard hearts, but this will last only until the full number of Gentiles comes to Christ. 26And so all Israel will be saved. As the Scriptures say,

"The one who rescues will come from Jerusalem,
and he will turn Israel away from ungodliness.
27 And this is my covenant with them,
that I will take away their sins."

28Many of the people of Israel are now enemies of the Good News, and this benefits you Gentiles. Yet they are still the people he loves because he chose their ancestors Abraham, Isaac, and Jacob. 29For God's gifts and his ʰcall can never be withdrawn. 30Once, you Gentiles were rebels against God, but when the people of Israel rebelled against him, God was merciful to you instead. 31Now they are the rebels, and God's mercy

has come to you so that they, too, will share in God's mercy. 32For God has imprisoned everyone in disobedience so he could have mercy on everyone.

Conclusion: Praise to God in Light of His Awesome Plan (11:33-36)

33Oh, how great are God's ⁱriches and wisdom and knowledge! How impossible it is for us to understand his decisions and his ways!

34 For who can know the LORD's thoughts?
    Who knows enough to give him advice?
35 And who has given him so much
    that he needs to pay it back?

36For everything comes from him and exists by his power and is intended for his glory. All glory to him forever! Amen.

5. THE TRANSFORMING POWER OF THE GOSPEL: CHRISTIAN CONDUCT (12:1–15:13)

The Heart of the Matter: Total Transformation (12:1-2)

12 And so, dear brothers and sisters, I plead with you to give your bodies to God because of all he has done for you. Let them be a living and holy sacrifice—the kind he will find acceptable. This is truly

Cross-references (right margin):

11:25 Luke 21:24
11:26-27 Ps 14:7 *Isa 59:20-21 Jer 31:31-34 Heb 8:8; 10:16
11:29 Heb 7:21 ʰklēsis (2821) ›1 Cor 1:2
11:32 Gal 3:22 1 Tim 2:4
11:33 Isa 45:15; 55:8 ⁱploutos (4149) ›Eph 1:7
11:34 Job 15:8; 36:22 *Isa 40:13 Jer 23:18 1 Cor 2:16
11:35 Job 41:11
11:36 1 Cor 8:6
12:1 1 Pet 2:5
12:2 Gal 1:4 Eph 4:23 Col 3:10 ⁱmetamorphoō (3339) ›2 Cor 3:18 ᵏthelēma (2307) ›Rom 15:32
12:3 Prov 3:7 1 Cor 12:11 Eph 4:7
12:4 1 Cor 12:12

---

vigor. By grafting wild olive branches (Gentiles) into the cultivated olive tree (the people of God), God has done what is contrary to nature.

11:25 dear brothers and sisters: Literally brothers. See note on 1:13. • Paul usually uses the word *mystery* to refer to an event of the last days that has already been determined by God. Such a *mystery* already exists in heaven, and is revealed to God's people in the Christian era (see 16:25; 1 Cor 2:1, 7; 4:1; 15:51; Eph 1:9; 3:3, 4, 9; 6:19; Col 1:26, 27; 2:2; 4:3; 1 Tim 3:9, 16). Here, the mystery is the relationship of Jews and *Gentiles* in the plan of salvation, which is at the heart of this entire passage (11:11-32).

11:26-27 The phrase *all Israel* could refer to the total of all believers, both Jewish and Gentile; with this meaning, *and so* would describe the way that God works to bring salvation to all his people. Alternatively, *all Israel* could refer to the total of all Jews destined to believe throughout the Christian era, or to a significant number of Jews who turn to Christ in the last days. With the last meaning, *and so* would have a sequential meaning—after the full number of Gentiles comes to Christ, *then* the full number of Jews will be saved. It does not mean all Jewish

people (see 2:17-29) • *As the Scriptures say:* This quotation is from Isa 59:20-21; 27:9 (Greek version). • In the OT, *The one who rescues* is the Lord. Paul almost surely is referring to Jesus Christ (see 1 Thes 1:10). • *from Jerusalem:* Greek *from Zion.* The Hebrew text of Isa 59:20 says that the redeemer will come *to* Jerusalem. Paul might have changed the wording to represent Jesus' first coming from among the people of Israel or to speak of the second coming when Jesus will return from the heavenly Jerusalem (see Heb 12:22). • *Israel:* Literally *Jacob.*

11:31 will share: Other manuscripts read *will now share;* still others read *will someday share.*

11:32 have mercy on everyone: *Everyone* has the sense of "all kinds of people." In the context of Romans, and especially this chapter, it refers to the inclusion of Gentiles alongside Jews.

11:34 This quotation is from Isa 40:13 (Greek version).

11:35 See Job 41:11.

11:36 everything comes from him and exists by his power: This statement is similar to statements found among Greek Stoic philosophers in their descriptions of God. Paul regularly draws on literature from the Greco-Roman world

to present and clarify the truth about God and his purposes (cp. Acts 17:24-29).

12:1–15:13 This section of Romans sets out the moral and ethical demands of the Good News. God's gift of salvation in Christ requires a response. God is not satisfied simply with forgiving our sin; he wants to transform our lives. Most of what Paul teaches concerning the moral duties of believers is paralleled in other letters. However, it also seems clear that he has chosen issues pertinent to the situation in Rome—most notably, the dispute between people who are weak in faith and people who are strong in faith (14:1–15:13).

12:1 dear brothers and sisters: Literally brothers. See note on 1:13. • *Your bodies* refers to the whole person in contact with the world, not just the physical body. • *because of all he has done for you:* As described in chs 1–11. • *This is truly the way to worship him* (or *This is your spiritual worship;* or *This is your reasonable service*): This phrase has at least three possible meanings: (1) Our sacrifice is *reasonable* in light of all God's mercies; (2) our sacrifice is *spiritual,* not the offering of an animal but of ourselves in spiritual service; or (3) our sacrifice is *intelligent,* offered with complete awareness of God's goodness to us.

12:5
1 Cor 12:27
Eph 4:25

12:6-8
1 Cor 12:4-11
1 Pet 4:10-11

12:6
ᵃ*charisma* (5486)
▸ 1 Cor 1:7

12:7
ᵇ*diakonia* (1248)
▸ 1 Cor 16:15

12:8
ᶜ*haplotēs* (0572)
▸ 2 Cor 8:2

12:9
Amos 5:15
1 Tim 1:5

12:10
John 13:34
Phil 2:3
1 Thes 4:9
2 Pet 1:7

12:12
Heb 10:32, 36

12:13
Heb 13:2

12:14
Matt 5:44

12:16
Prov 3:7
Isa 5:21

the way to worship him. ²Don't copy the behavior and customs of this world, but let God ʲtransform you into a new person by changing the way you think. Then you will learn to know God's ᵏwill for you, which is good and pleasing and perfect.

Humility and Mutual Service (12:3-8)

³Because of the privilege and authority God has given me, I give each of you this warning: Don't think you are better than you really are. Be honest in your evaluation of yourselves, measuring yourselves by the faith God has given us. ⁴Just as our bodies have many parts and each part has a special function, ⁵so it is with Christ's body. We are many parts of one body, and we all belong to each other.

⁶In his grace, God has given us different ᵃgifts for doing certain things well. So if God has given you the ability to prophesy, speak out with as much faith as God has given you. ⁷If your gift is ᵇserving others, ᵇserve them well. If you are a teacher, teach well. ⁸If your gift is to encourage others, be encouraging. If it is giving, give ᶜgenerously. If God has given you leadership ability, take the responsibility seriously. And if you have a gift for showing kindness to others, do it gladly.

Love and Its Manifestations (12:9-21)

⁹Don't just pretend to love others. Really love them. Hate what is wrong. Hold tightly to what is good. ¹⁰Love each other with genuine affection, and take delight in honoring each other. ¹¹Never be lazy, but work hard and serve the Lord enthusiastically. ¹²Rejoice in our confident hope. Be patient in trouble, and keep on praying. ¹³When God's people are in need, be ready to help them. Always be eager to practice hospitality.

¹⁴Bless those who persecute you. Don't curse them; pray that God will bless them. ¹⁵Be happy with those who are happy, and weep with those who weep. ¹⁶Live in harmony with each other. Don't be too proud to enjoy the company of ordinary people. And don't think you know it all!

. . . .

12:2 *this world* (literally *this age*): The division of history into two ages was typical of the Jewish worldview. Early Christians adapted this point of view, identifying the coming of Christ as the time when the new age of salvation began. Unexpectedly, however, the new age did not bring an end to the old age. The old way of thinking and living continues, and is a source of temptation even to Christians who seek to conform their lives to the values of the new age.

12:3 *Because of the privilege and authority:* Or *Because of the grace;* cp. 1:5. • *by the faith God has given us:* Or *by the faith God has given you;* or *by the standard of our God-given faith.* Whether Paul is referring to the amount of faith each of us has been given or to the Christian faith that we all hold in common, we need to assess ourselves accurately by this measure and not be vain about the abilities God has given us.

12:4-5 *so it is with Christ's body:* The parallel between the human body and the church—the body of Christ—is also found in 1 Cor 12. This metaphor provides an effective picture of unity and diversity in the church (cp. Livy, *History* 2.32; Epictetus, *Discourses* 2.10.4–5).

12:6 *The ability to prophesy* was one of the most important of the NT gifts (see also 1 Cor 12:28; Eph 4:11). Although prophets are mentioned in several passages in Acts as predicting the future (see Acts 11:28; 21:10-12), the prophet's most fundamental responsibility is to communicate God's message to the community of believers (1 Cor 12:3, 24-

25, 29-30; see also 1 Cor 14). • *as much faith as God has given you* (literally *in proportion to the faith*): *Proportion* (Greek *analogia*) is a word drawn from mathematics and logic, where it refers to the correct proportions in a relationship among things, quantities, or ideas. Paul uses the phrase to remind prophets to make sure that their utterances are in right proportion to faith, whether the amount of individual faith the prophet has been given, or the Christian faith in general (see note on 12:3). This passage has given theology the phrase *the analogy of faith,* which refers to the importance of bringing the interpretation of any particular passage into line with the teaching of all of Scripture.

12:7 *teacher:* The gift of teaching comes third in the list of gifts in 1 Cor 12:28 and fifth in Eph 4:11. While prophets communicate to the community a message received directly from God, teachers address the church on the basis of studying the word of God.

12:8 *give generously:* See also 2 Cor 8:2; 9:11, 13.

12:9-21 The many injunctions in these verses do not follow a neat logical arrangement. The overall topic, stated at the beginning, is sincere *love.* Paul shows how we are to love both those inside the church (12:10, 13, 15-16) and those outside the church (12:14, 17-21).

12:10 *with genuine affection:* Literally *with brotherly love.* The key Greek word in this phrase connotes love of family. Christians are to *love each other* with the mutual love and commitment that are found within a healthy family.

12:11 *but work hard and serve the Lord enthusiastically* (or *but serve the Lord with a zealous spirit;* or *but let the Spirit excite you as you serve the Lord*): As Christians, we are to be passionate about our faith and eager to fulfill our ministry to others within the church.

12:12 The three commands in this verse are related. By rejoicing in *confident hope,* we can *be patient in trouble.* Continually *praying* is essential if we desire to have this attitude toward the difficulties of life (see also 8:24-27).

12:13 *be ready to help them:* The verb Paul uses is related to the familiar Greek word *koinōnia* ("fellowship"). When needs arise among our Christian brothers and sisters, we are not just to meet their needs; we should also enter into fellowship with these fellow Christians in ways that extend beyond material gifts.

12:14 The exhortations in this verse closely resemble two sayings of Jesus (Matt 5:44; Luke 6:27-28). Although Paul does not introduce the commands as a quotation, he is almost certainly alluding to these sayings of Christ. Perhaps the words were so well-known that he did not need to specify the source. The teaching of Rom 12–13 has many parallels with the teaching of Jesus.

12:16 All three exhortations in this verse use the Greek word *phroneō* (*think*). Paul addresses the need for right Christian thinking when it comes to our relationships with other Christians. • *Live in harmony:* Literally *Think the same things.* • *Don't be too proud:* Literally *Don't think arrogant things.*

¹⁷Never pay back evil with more evil. Do things in such a way that everyone can see you are honorable. ¹⁸Do all that you can to live in peace with everyone.

¹⁹Dear friends, never take revenge. Leave that to the righteous anger of God. For the Scriptures say,

"I will take revenge;
I will pay them back,"
says the LORD.

²⁰Instead,

"If your enemies are hungry, feed them.
If they are thirsty, give them
something to drink.
In doing this, you will heap
burning coals of shame on their heads."

²¹Don't let evil conquer you, but conquer evil by doing good.

The Christian and Secular Rulers (13:1-7)

13 Everyone must submit to governing authorities. For all authority comes from God, and those in positions of authority have been placed there by God. ²So anyone who rebels against authority is rebelling against what God has instituted, and they will be punished. ³For the authorities do not strike fear in people who are doing right, but in those who are doing wrong. Would you like to live without fear of the authorities? Do what is right, and they will honor you. ⁴The authorities are God's servants, sent for your good. But if you are doing wrong, of course you should be afraid, for they have the power to punish you. They are God's servants, sent for the very purpose of punishing those who do what is wrong. ⁵So you must submit to them, not only to avoid punishment, but also to keep a clear conscience.

⁶Pay your taxes, too, for these same reasons. For government workers need to be paid. They are ᵈserving God in what they do. ⁷Give to everyone what you owe them: Pay your taxes and government fees to those who collect them, and give respect and honor to those who are in authority.

Love and the Law (13:8-10)

⁸Owe nothing to anyone—except for your obligation to love one another. If you love your neighbor, you will fulfill the

12:17
Prov 3:4; 20:22
1 Thes 5:15

12:19
*Deut 32:35

12:20
*Prov 25:21-22
Matt 5:44

13:1
Dan 2:21
John 19:11
Titus 3:1

13:3
1 Pet 2:13-14

13:5
1 Pet 2:13

13:6
ᵈ*leitourgos* (3011)
▸ Rom 15:16

13:7
Matt 22:21
Mark 12:17
Luke 20:25

13:8
Matt 5:43
John 13:34

13:9
Exod 20:13-15, 17
*Lev 19:18
Deut 5:17-19, 21

. . . .

12:18 *Do all that you can:* Paul recognizes that our efforts to live at peace with others will sometimes be frustrated by our own moral constraints or by other peoples' unwillingness to be reconciled to us.

12:19 This quotation is from Deut 32:35.

12:20-21 A simple act of Christian kindness can often bring a hostile person to repentance before God and restore fellowship between people.

12:20 This quotation is from Prov 25:21-22.

13:1-2 The basic command of 13:1-7 is to *submit to governing authorities.* In God's ordering of the world, we answer to *those in positions of authority.* Our submission to them will usually take the form of obedience. However, because God stands over all governments, our submission to governing authorities must always be in terms of our ultimate submission to God (see Acts 4:19-20). The Roman Christians might have been resisting government (see note on 13:6) based on a false understanding of the Good News, as if no longer copying "the behavior and customs of this world" (12:2) meant that they could ignore earthly institutions. • *placed there by God:* Scripture consistently teaches that God is actively involved in raising up and casting down human governments (1 Sam 2:6-10; 12:8; Prov 8:15-16; Isa 41:2-4; 45:1-7; Jer 21:7, 10; 27:5-6; Dan 2:21, 37-38; 4:17). God instituted governing authorities, so rebelling against them is rebelling against God,

who will respond with judgment (13:2).

13:3 *the authorities do not strike fear in people who are doing right:* Paul presents a positive picture of the governing authorities, describing them in terms of what God has appointed them to do. He does not touch on situations where leaders punish those who do good and reward those who do evil, although he was certainly aware of such situations from OT and Jewish history, from the experience of Jesus and the other apostles, and from Greco-Roman affairs. Here, Paul confines himself to discussing the appropriate response to governing authorities who live according to their calling.

13:4 *servants* (Greek *diakonos*): The NT usually reserves this word to describe Christians who serve God in various capacities. However, it was also used in secular Greek to refer to a civic official. Whether they know it or not, governing authorities are serving God when they administer justice. • *they have the power to punish you* (literally *they do not bear the sword in vain*): The *sword* might simply be a metaphor for punishment of any kind, but some interpreters believe it suggests that human governments, under God's authority, have the right to carry out capital punishment.

13:5 The two reasons for submission sum up the argument of 13:1-4 in reverse order: *to avoid punishment* relates to 13:3-4, while *to keep a clear conscience* refers to 13:1-2. • The word *conscience* (Greek *suneidēsis*) refers to

the painful knowledge of wrongdoing. Christians know about their duty to submit to governing authorities, and their failure to do so would bring the pain of a guilty conscience.

13:6 *Pay your taxes:* Jesus referred to paying taxes in his famous pronouncement about the disciples' relationship to government (Matt 22:21). A tax revolt occurred in Rome at about the time that Paul was writing, so Paul's whole discussion of the Christian's responsibility to government might have been sparked by his knowledge that Roman Christians were participating in this tax revolt (see Tacitus, *Annals* 13).

13:8-10 These verses discuss how believers relate to other people. If we truly love others, our actions will reflect all the commandments in the law that concern our relationships with other people.

13:8 The idea of *obligation* is the hinge that connects 13:1-7 and 13:8-10. Christians are to "give to everyone what [they] owe them" (13:7); and Christians always owe love to their neighbors. • *Owe nothing to anyone:* Debts are not sinful but should be avoided and, if incurred, should be promptly repaid so that the believer is free to serve in love (see Prov 22:7). • *love one another:* Believers are called to love all those they encounter (12:14-21; Luke 10:25-37), but the phrase especially emphasizes the love that each believer owes to other believers. • *you will fulfill the requirements of God's law:* This teaching closely follows Jesus' teaching in Matt 22:34-40.

13:10
Matt 22:39
John 13:34-35
Gal 5:13-14
ᵉagapē (0026)
  ▸ Rom 14:15

13:11
1 Cor 7:29-31
1 Thes 5:5-6
Jas 5:8
1 Pet 4:7

13:12
Eph 5:11; 6:13
1 Thes 5:8

13:13
Luke 21:34
Eph 5:18

14:1
1 Cor 9:22
ᶠpistis (4102)
  ▸ Gal 2:20

14:2
1 Cor 10:25-27

14:3
Col 2:16

14:4
Matt 7:1

14:5
Gal 4:10

14:6
1 Cor 10:30

14:7
2 Cor 5:15
Gal 2:20

14:8
Phil 1:20
1 Thes 5:10

14:9
Rev 1:18

requirements of God's law. ⁹For the commandments say, "You must not commit adultery. You must not murder. You must not steal. You must not covet." These—and other such commandments—are summed up in this one commandment: "Love your neighbor as yourself." ¹⁰ᵉLove does no wrong to others, so ᵉlove fulfills the requirements of God's law.

Living in Light of the Day (13:11-14)

¹¹This is all the more urgent, for you know how late it is; time is running out. Wake up, for our salvation is nearer now than when we first believed. ¹²The night is almost gone; the day of salvation will soon be here. So remove your dark deeds like dirty clothes, and put on the shining armor of right living. ¹³Because we belong to the day, we must live decent lives for all to see. Don't participate in the darkness of wild parties and drunkenness, or in sexual promiscuity and immoral living, or in quarreling and jealousy. ¹⁴Instead, clothe yourself with the presence of the Lord Jesus Christ. And don't let yourself think about ways to indulge your evil desires.

A Plea for Unity (14:1–15:13)
Do Not Condemn One Another!

14 Accept other believers who are weak in ᶠfaith, and don't argue with them about what they think is right or wrong. ²For instance, one person believes it's all right to eat anything. But another believer with a sensitive conscience will eat only vegetables. ³Those who feel free to eat anything must not look down on those who don't. And those who don't eat certain foods must not condemn those who do, for God has accepted them. ⁴Who are you to condemn someone else's servants? Their own master will judge whether they stand or fall. And with the Lord's help, they will stand and receive his approval.

⁵In the same way, some think one day is more holy than another day, while others think every day is alike. You should each be fully convinced that whichever day you choose is acceptable. ⁶Those who worship the Lord on a special day do it to honor him. Those who eat any kind of food do so to honor the Lord, since they give thanks to God before eating. And those who refuse to eat certain foods also want to please the Lord and give thanks to God. ⁷For we don't live for ourselves or die for ourselves. ⁸If we live, it's to honor the Lord. And if we die, it's to honor the Lord. So whether we live or die, we belong to the Lord. ⁹Christ died and rose again for this very purpose—to be Lord both of the living and of the dead.

. . . .

13:9 *"You must not commit adultery. . . . You must not covet":* This quotation is from Exod 20:13-15, 17. • *"Love your neighbor as yourself":* This quotation is from Lev 19:18.

13:11 The NT often speaks of *salvation* as the final victory over sin and death that believers will experience when Jesus returns in glory (see 5:9-10).

13:12-13 *the day of salvation:* The word *day* reflects two sources. First, the OT repeatedly predicts the *day of the Lord* when God's plan culminates (see Isa 13:4-13; Jer 30:8-9; Joel 2:32; 3:18; Obad 1:15-18). Second, the tradition of moral instruction in the ancient world associated light/daytime with good and darkness/nighttime with evil. The Greeks, Romans, and ancient Jews all used this contrast. Because believers *belong to the day* they should be living out its values, avoiding the *dark deeds* that are typical of nighttime.

14:1–15:7 Paul moves to a specific issue that was causing conflict in the church at Rome. The church in Rome was embroiled in a dispute between people who were *weak in faith* and people who were *strong* (see 15:1) regarding certain practices. Throughout this section, Paul instructs believers to be tolerant toward others and their practices; he is convinced that people

on both sides of the issue are genuine believers, and he does not think the issues they are fighting over are essential to the faith.

14:1 Being *weak in faith* means having scruples against doing certain things that Christian liberty would allow. In Rome, most of the weak in faith were Jewish Christians whose consciences did not give them liberty from certain requirements of Jewish law.

14:2 The weak in faith apparently believed that they should *eat only vegetables.* Their conviction probably stemmed from a concern to maintain Jewish ritual purity in the midst of a pagan culture. These Jewish Christians were following the lead of Daniel and his friends, who refused to eat the rich food and wine that the king of Babylon offered them (Dan 1:3-16). Other Jewish sources reveal that pious Jews often restricted their diets in pagan cultures because they could never be sure that meat had been slaughtered according to Jewish requirements.

14:3-4 *look down on . . . condemn:* The "strong," those who prided themselves on their enlightened freedom in Christ, looked with disdain on those they considered to be "weak." The weak, in turn—certain that they were following the true route to piety—condemned

the strong for their laxness. These attitudes, over different issues, are mirrored throughout the history of the Christian church. • *God has accepted them:* Both the weak and the strong are genuine believers, welcomed by God into his family. Therefore, they have no right to treat each other as if they do not belong (14:4; see also 15:7).

14:5 *some think one day is more holy than another day, while others think every day is alike:* The reference is probably to Jewish festival days and to the Sabbath; cp. Col 2:16. With Christ's provision of salvation, observance of the Sabbath in its original form is not required of Christians.

14:7 As the Lord's servants (14:4), Christians are to look to God for guidance and seek to honor him in all things (14:8). Because we are ultimately accountable to him, our desire should always be to please him, not to *live for ourselves.*

14:9 Paul refers to standard early Christian teaching on the significance of Jesus' death and resurrection (e.g., 2 Cor 5:15). • *of the living and of the dead* (literally *of the dead and of the living*): The original word order matches the sequence of Jesus' death and resurrection, the redemptive events that make Jesus our Lord.

[10]So why do you condemn another believer? Why do you look down on another believer? Remember, we will all stand before the judgment seat of God. [11]For the Scriptures say,

" 'As surely as I live,' says the LORD,
'every knee will bend to me,
    and every [g]tongue will confess and
        give praise to God.' "

[12]Yes, each of us will give a personal [h]account to God.

Do Not Cause Your Brother or Sister to Stumble!

[13]So let's stop condemning each other. Decide instead to live in such a way that you will not cause another believer to [i]stumble and fall.

[14]I know and am convinced on the authority of the Lord Jesus that no food, in and of itself, is wrong to eat. But if someone believes it is wrong, then for that person it is wrong. [15]And if another believer is distressed by what you eat, you are not acting in [j]love if you eat it. Don't let your eating ruin someone for whom Christ died. [16]Then you will not be criticized for doing something you believe is good. [17]For the Kingdom of God is not a matter of what we eat or drink, but of living a life of goodness and peace and joy in the Holy Spirit. [18]If you serve Christ with this attitude, you will please God, and others will approve of you, too. [19]So then, let us aim for [k]harmony in the church and try to build each other up.

[20]Don't tear apart the work of God over what you eat. Remember, all foods are acceptable, but it is wrong to eat something if it makes another person [a]stumble. [21]It is better not to eat meat or drink wine or do anything else if it might cause another believer to stumble. [22]You may believe there's nothing wrong with what you are doing, but keep it between yourself and God. Blessed are those who don't feel guilty for doing something they have decided is right. [23]But if you have doubts about whether or not you should eat something, you are sinning if you go ahead and do it. For you are not following your convictions. If you do anything you believe is not right, you are [b]sinning.

Put Other People First!

15 We who are strong must be considerate of those who are sensitive about

14:10
2 Cor 5:10
14:11
*Isa 45:23; 49:18
[g]glōssa (1100)
▸ 1 Cor 12:10
14:12
Gal 6:5
[h]logos (3056)
▸ Rom 15:18
14:13
Matt 7:1
[i]proskomma (4348)
▸ Rom 14:20
14:14
Acts 10:15
1 Cor 8:7
14:15
1 Cor 8:11-13
[j]agapē (0026)
▸ 1 Cor 8:1
14:16
1 Cor 10:30
14:17
Gal 5:22
14:19
[k]eirēnē (1515)
▸ 1 Cor 14:33
14:20
Acts 10:15
1 Cor 8:9-12
[a]proskomma (4348)
▸ 1 Cor 1:23
14:21
1 Cor 8:13
14:22
1 Jn 3:21
14:23
[b]hamartia (0266)
▸ 1 Cor 15:56

. . . .

14:10 *another believer:* Literally *your brother;* also in 14:10b, 13, 15, 21. See note on 1:13. • *we will all stand before the judgment seat of God:* Paul reminds the Roman Christians that it is God, not other Christians, who will ultimately judge all of us (cp. 2 Cor 5:10).

14:11 This quotation is from Isa 49:18; 45:23 (Greek version). In its original context, Isa 45:23 is surrounded by assertions of God's sovereignty (Isa 45:22, 24). Only the sovereign God has the right to stand in judgment (14:10, 12). • *confess and give praise to God:* Or *confess allegiance to God.*

14:13 This verse acts as a bridge. *Let's stop condemning each other* summarizes 14:1-12, while the concern about causing *another believer to stumble and fall* becomes the major emphasis of 14:14-23. • *stumble and fall:* This phrase originally applied to obstacles that could trip people as they walked, or to traps into which a person might fall. It is used metaphorically throughout the NT for behavior that might bring spiritual harm to another person (see 1 Cor 8:9, 13; 1 Jn 2:10; cp. Matt 21:42-44; Luke 20:17-18; Rom 9:32-33; 1 Pet 2:8).

14:14 *no food, in and of itself, is wrong to eat* (literally *nothing is common in itself*): The word *common* signals that the root concern that Paul was addressing was Jewish purity regulations. Jews described food as *common* if it was not clean (i.e., not kosher), thereby causing a Jew to become ritually impure (see Lev 11; cp. Mark 7:2, 5; Acts 10:14). Paul again follows the teaching of Jesus that "every kind of food is acceptable in God's eyes" (Mark 7:19). • *for that person it is wrong:* The truth that no food is wrong to eat was not easy for pious Jews to accept because they had been raised to honor God by avoiding certain foods. Paul urges those who are strong in faith not to force others to violate their consciences (cp. 1 Cor 8:1-13).

14:15 The word translated *ruin* (Greek *apollumi,* "destroy") is often applied to eternal damnation (see 2:12; Matt 10:28; 18:14; Luke 9:24; 13:2-5; John 3:16; 10:10, 28; 1 Cor 1:18-19; Jas 4:12; 2 Pet 3:9). By insisting on their freedom to eat whatever they want, the strong might cause sensitive Jewish Christians *for whom Christ died* to turn away from the faith.

14:20 *The work of God* refers both to the spiritual life of other Christians (14:15) and to the Christian community itself (14:19). The strong, with their dogged insistence on doing whatever they want, create division and disrupt God's intention to build a healthy and united community of believers.

14:21 *or drink wine:* Jews sometimes abstained from wine to avoid the appearance of ritual contamination, since wine was used in pagan religious celebrations (see Dan 1:3-16).

14:22 *keep it between yourself and God:* Paul did not contest the freedom of the strong believers, but he instructed them to limit the expression of their freedom out of love for fellow believers so that the whole Christian community could be built up. • *Blessed are those who don't feel guilty:* Guilt could come from harming the faith of the weak believers. Christian freedom is only worthwhile when it can be lived out without bringing such guilt.

14:23 *If you do anything you believe is not right, you are sinning:* God's word defines sin for us, yet sin also involves violating our conscience. The weak Christians in Rome did not yet believe in their own hearts that they could eat meat, drink wine, or ignore Jewish holy days; their consciences were still weak. They should not violate their consciences on these matters. Nor should the strong, by the power of their example or by their scorn, force weak Christians to do so.

15:1-4 *We who are strong:* Paul aligns himself with those he identifies as strong in faith, and he reveals that the division in the Roman church was not simply between Jews and Gentiles. Like Paul, some Jews had enlightened consciences and so were counted

15:2
1 Cor 9:19; 10:24
Gal 6:2

15:3
*Ps 69:9

15:4
2 Tim 3:16
ᶜ*paraklēsis* (3874)
▸1 Cor 14:31

15:5
1 Cor 1:10
2 Cor 1:3

15:6
Rev 1:6

15:8
Matt 15:24
Acts 3:25-26
2 Cor 1:20

15:9
*2 Sam 22:50
*Ps 18:49

things like this. We must not just please ourselves. ²We should help others do what is right and build them up in the Lord. ³For even Christ didn't live to please himself. As the Scriptures say, "The insults of those who insult you, O God, have fallen on me." ⁴Such things were written in the Scriptures long ago to teach us. And the Scriptures give us hope and ᶜencouragement as we wait patiently for God's promises to be fulfilled.

⁵May God, who gives this patience and encouragement, help you live in complete harmony with each other, as is fitting for followers of Christ Jesus. ⁶Then all of you can join together with one voice, giving praise and glory to God, the Father of our Lord Jesus Christ.

Receive One Another!

⁷Therefore, accept each other just as Christ has accepted you so that God will be given glory. ⁸Remember that Christ came as a servant to the Jews to show that God is true to the promises he made to their ancestors. ⁹He also came so that the Gentiles might give glory to God for his mercies to them. That is what the psalmist meant when he wrote:

"For this, I will praise you among the
Gentiles;
I will sing praises to your name."

. . . .

Tolerance and Its Limits (14:1–15:13)

Rom 12:9-21
Ps 133:1-3
1 Cor 1:10; 6:1-20;
8:1-13; 10:1–11:1;
12:12-27; 13:1-8
2 Cor 6:14–7:1
Col 3:12-15
2 Tim 2:23-26

Paul pleads for tolerance between those who are weak in faith and those who are strong in faith, and he teaches that believers need to accept each other (14:1; 15:7). They should stop condemning and belittling each other. Rather, they should learn to worship God with a united voice and spirit (15:6).

Paul is addressing the specific issue of whether believers need to practice certain requirements of the OT law and of Jewish worship. Theologians have used the word *adiaphora* ("non-essentials") to describe beliefs or practices that are neither required nor prohibited by Scripture. On such issues, Christians must accommodate a variety of opinions.

Paul takes a very different approach when the Good News itself is at stake. In Galatians, for example, Paul confronts false teaching about the Good News by severely castigating the false teachers (Gal 1:6-9) and by warning readers that adopting false teaching will alienate them from Christ (Gal 5:4).

In our day, we need to be careful about what we tolerate and accommodate, and we need to be equally careful about what we decide is worthy of confrontation. Believers need to consider carefully the different issues they confront in their associations with other believers. If the basic truth of the Good News is not violated, we should not quarrel or be divided over such issues. Other issues, however, strike at the heart of the message of Good News. In these cases, Christians need to take a stand and be faithful to the Good News and to Christ. The way Paul himself dealt with a variety of issues in his own time can serve as a guide for dealing with conflicts and controversies in our time.

. . . .

among the strong. Similarly, some Gentiles were so strongly influenced by Jewish teaching and tradition that they were among the weak in faith.
• *must be considerate of those who are sensitive about things like this:* This phrase is reminiscent of Gal 6:2. Paul did not want the strong to simply put up with those who were weak in faith; rather the strong were to actively and sympathetically assist the weak in living out their Christian faith with integrity (see also Gal 5:13-15).

15:2 *others* (literally *the neighbor*): See Lev 19:18, quoted in 13:9. Love for others should govern the conduct of people who are strong in faith.

15:3 This quotation is from Ps 69:9.
• A number of passages in the NT use Psalm 69 to describe Jesus' suffering (Matt 27:34; Mark 15:35-36; Luke 23:36; John 15:25; 19:28-29). Paul's quotation

of just a small portion of that psalm evokes the whole experience of Jesus' suffering. • *who insult you, O God, have fallen on me:* Literally *who insult you have fallen on me.*

15:4 *Such things were written in the Scriptures long ago to teach us:* All that God caused to be recorded in the OT has supreme relevance to believers, who experience the fulfillment of God's plan.

15:5-6 *live in complete harmony:* This phrase (see note on 12:16) refers to the whole orientation of how someone thinks. A mindset of harmony is important for Christian unity (see 12:3-5, 16; Phil 2:2-5).

15:7 To *accept each other* means more than grudgingly putting up with each other. We are to welcome other believers, with all their flaws and sins, into our fellowship and treat them

as family (see note on 12:10), *just as Christ has accepted* us, with all our flaws and sins, into his fellowship and family (5:8-11).

15:8-9 Through *Christ,* God made it possible for *Jews* and *Gentiles* to join together to give glory to God in the new covenant people of God (see chs 9–11). The issue of Jewish–Gentile relationships was fundamental to the dispute in the Roman church (14:1–15:7).

15:8 *servant to the Jews:* Literally *servant of circumcision.*

15:9-12 These quotations from the OT all emphasize God's promise that *Gentiles* would join with Jews in praising God. Gentiles are now full members of God's people.

15:9 This quotation is from Ps 18:49.

¹⁰And in another place it is written,

"Rejoice with his people,
you Gentiles."

¹¹And yet again,

"Praise the LORD, all you Gentiles.
Praise him, all you people of the
earth."

¹²And in another place Isaiah said,

"The heir to David's throne will come,
and he will rule over the Gentiles.
They will place their hope on him."

¹³I pray that God, the source of hope, will fill you completely with joy and peace because you trust in him. Then you will overflow with confident hope through the power of the Holy Spirit.

6. THE LETTER CLOSING (15:14–16:27)
Paul's Ministry and Travel Plans
¹⁴I am fully convinced, my dear brothers and sisters, that you are full of ᵈgoodness. You know these things so well you can teach each other all about them. ¹⁵Even so, I have been bold enough to write about some of these points, knowing that all you need is this reminder. For by God's grace, ¹⁶I am a ᵉspecial messenger from Christ Jesus to you Gentiles. I bring you the Good News so that I might present you as an acceptable offering to God, made holy by the Holy Spirit.

¹⁷So I have reason to be enthusiastic about all Christ Jesus has done through me in my service to God. ¹⁸Yet I dare not boast about anything except what Christ has done through me, bringing the Gentiles to God by my ᶠmessage and by the way I worked among them. ¹⁹They were convinced by the power of miraculous ᵍsigns and wonders and by the power of God's Spirit. In this way, I have fully presented the ʰGood News of Christ from Jerusalem all the way to Illyricum.

²⁰My ambition has always been to preach the Good News where the name of Christ has never been heard, rather than where a church has already been started by someone else. ²¹I have been following the plan spoken of in the Scriptures, where it says,

"Those who have never been told about
him will see,
and those who have never heard of
him will understand."

²²In fact, my visit to you has been delayed so long because I have been preaching in these places.

²³But now I have finished my work in these regions, and after all these long years of waiting, I am eager to visit you. ²⁴I am planning to go to Spain, and when I do, I will stop off in Rome. And after I have enjoyed your fellowship for a little while, you can provide for my journey.

15:10
*Deut 32:43
15:11
*Ps 117:1
15:12
*Isa 11:10
Rev 5:5; 22:16
15:14
2 Pet 1:12
ᵈ*agathōsunē* (0019)
‣ Gal 5:22
15:15
Rom 1:5; 12:3
15:16
Phil 2:17
ᵉ*leitourgos* (3011)
‣ 2 Cor 9:12
15:17
Phil 3:3
15:18
Rom 1:5
ᶠ*logos* (3056)
‣ Gal 5:14
15:19
Acts 19:11
1 Cor 2:4
1 Thes 1:5
ᵍ*sēmeion* (4592)
‣ 1 Cor 1:22
ʰ*euangelion* (2098)
‣ 1 Cor 15:1
15:20
Rom 1:15
1 Cor 3:10
2 Cor 10:13, 15
15:21
*Isa 52:15
15:22
Rom 1:10-13
1 Thes 2:18
15:23
Acts 19:21
Rom 1:10-11
15:24
1 Cor 16:6

. . . .

15:10 This quotation is from Deut 32:43.

15:11 This quotation is from Ps 117:1.

15:12 This quotation is from Isa 11:10 (Greek version). • *The heir to David's throne:* Literally *The root of Jesse.* David was the son of Jesse.

15:14–16:27 This final section contains elements common at the end of NT letters: a discussion of travel plans (15:14-29), requests for prayer (15:30-33), references to ministry associates (16:1-2, 21-23), greetings (16:3-16), and a doxology (16:25-27). Only the warning about false teachers (16:17-19) is a non-standard feature in this conclusion.

15:14 *dear brothers and sisters:* Literally *brothers;* also in 15:30. See note on 1:13. • *You know these things so well:* Paul praises the Roman Christians, as he had in the opening of the letter (see 1:8-12), demonstrating a gracious manner toward a church he had neither founded nor visited.

15:15-16 *by God's grace:* Paul emphasized that his role as apostle and teacher was because God had chosen

him to lead in the formation of the Christian church (see also 1:5; 12:3; 1 Cor 3:10; Gal 2:9; Eph 3:2, 7, 8).

15:16 *special messenger:* The Greek word (*leitourgos,* "servant" or "minister") could refer to almost any kind of servant, but Jews often applied the word to priests. Paul probably chose this word to emphasize the priestly nature of his ministry. • *to you Gentiles:* Paul stresses the Gentile flavor of the church in Rome (see also 1:6-7). This does not mean that there were no Jews in the church (see 16:3-16), but Gentiles had become the majority. • *present you as an acceptable offering to God:* Paul was fulfilling Isa 66:19-20.

15:19 *God's Spirit:* Other manuscripts read *the Spirit;* still others read *the Holy Spirit.* • *I have fully presented the Good News of Christ:* Paul was not claiming that the work of evangelism had been completed in these regions. His point was that churches had been planted in enough major population centers so that those churches could carry on the work of evangelism themselves. Paul's own distinctive ministry of planting foundational and strategic churches had been fulfilled. • *from*

Jerusalem all the way to Illyricum: Illyricum was a region northeast of Italy, a Roman province that occupied most of the coastlands along the Adriatic Sea, from modern-day Albania to Croatia. An arc drawn from Jerusalem to Illyricum would include the areas where Paul had planted churches (southern Galatia, Asia Minor, Macedonia, and Greece).

15:21 This quotation is from Isa 52:15 (Greek version).

15:24 *I am planning to go to Spain:* In Paul's day, "Spain" included the entire Iberian Peninsula (modern Spain and Portugal). Parts of the peninsula had been occupied by the Romans since 200 BC, but only within Paul's lifetime had the area been organized into a Roman province. Paul saw Spain, at the far end of the Mediterranean, as his final target in fulfilling the promise of Isa 66:19-20. • *you can provide for my journey:* Spain was so far from Paul's previous sending church, Antioch in Syria, that he hoped the Roman church could serve as the logistical base for this future evangelistic effort.

15:25
Acts 19:21; 20:22

15:26
1 Cor 16:1
2 Cor 8:1; 9:2

15:27
1 Cor 9:11

15:29
Rom 1:10-11

15:30
2 Cor 1:11
Col 1:8; 4:12

15:31
2 Thes 3:2

15:32
Phlm 1:7
ᶦthelēma (2307)
▸ Eph 6:6

15:33
Rom 16:20
Heb 13:20

16:1
Acts 18:18
ᶦdiakonos (1249)
▸ 2 Cor 11:23

16:2
Phil 2:29

16:5
1 Cor 16:15, 19
Col 4:15
Phlm 1:2
ᵏekklēsia (1577)
▸ 1 Cor 1:2

16:7
Rom 16:11, 21
Col 4:10
Phlm 1:23

²⁵But before I come, I must go to Jerusalem to take a gift to the believers there. ²⁶For you see, the believers in Macedonia and Achaia have eagerly taken up an offering for the poor among the believers in Jerusalem. ²⁷They were glad to do this because they feel they owe a real debt to them. Since the Gentiles received the spiritual blessings of the Good News from the believers in Jerusalem, they feel the least they can do in return is to help them financially. ²⁸As soon as I have delivered this money and completed this good deed of theirs, I will come to see you on my way to Spain. ²⁹And I am sure that when I come, Christ will richly bless our time together.

³⁰Dear brothers and sisters, I urge you in the name of our Lord Jesus Christ to join in my struggle by praying to God for me. Do this because of your love for me, given to you by the Holy Spirit. ³¹Pray that I will be rescued from those in Judea who refuse to obey God. Pray also that the believers there will be willing to accept the donation I am taking to Jerusalem. ³²Then, by the ᶦwill of God, I will be able to come to you with a joyful heart, and we will be an encouragement to each other.

³³And now may God, who gives us his peace, be with you all. Amen.

Paul Greets His Friends

16 I commend to you our sister Phoebe, who is a ᶦdeacon in the church in Cenchrea. ²Welcome her in the Lord as one who is worthy of honor among God's people. Help her in whatever she needs, for she has been helpful to many, and especially to me.

³Give my greetings to Priscilla and Aquila, my co-workers in the ministry of Christ Jesus. ⁴In fact, they once risked their lives for me. I am thankful to them, and so are all the Gentile churches. ⁵Also give my greetings to the ᵏchurch that meets in their home.

Greet my dear friend Epenetus. He was the first person from the province of Asia to become a follower of Christ. ⁶Give my greetings to Mary, who has worked so hard for your benefit. ⁷Greet Andronicus

. . . .

15:25-28 *I must go to Jerusalem to take a gift to the believers there:* During his third missionary journey, Paul collected donations from the Gentile churches to help the believers in Jerusalem and to draw the two wings of the first-century church closer together (see also 1 Cor 16:1-2; 2 Cor 8–9).

15:25 *the believers:* Literally *God's holy people;* also in 15:26, 31.

15:26 *Macedonia* and *Achaia* were the northern and southern regions of Greece. Paul founded churches in several prominent cities in Macedonia, including Philippi, Thessalonica, and Berea. In Achaia, Paul had preached in Athens and founded the church in Corinth (see Acts 16–18). • *the poor among the believers in Jerusalem:* Jewish Christians in Jerusalem were suffering from famines that had hit the area (see Acts 11:27-30), and also because their faith in Christ caused them to be ostracized from Jewish society.

15:27 *they owe a real debt:* Gentile Christians owe their spiritual existence to God's work among the Israelites (see 11:17-24).

15:31 *Pray that I will be rescued from those in Judea who refuse to obey God:* See Acts 21–22. God preserved Paul's life and used the circumstances of his arrest in Jerusalem to take him precisely where he planned to go—Rome. • *the donation:* Literally *the ministry;* other manuscripts read *the gift.*

15:33 Some manuscripts do not include *Amen.* One very early manuscript places the doxology (16:25-27) here. This has led some scholars to conclude that the original letter to the Romans consisted of only 1:1–15:33, but few now follow this theory. The best early manuscripts place the doxology at the end of ch 16, and the whole of ch 16 was most likely part of Paul's original letter to the Romans. See also note on 16:1-6.

16:1-16 Paul here commended and greeted twenty-seven Roman Christians, ten of whom were women. Women played important roles in the early church. • Paul had never been to Rome, which has led to some speculation as to how he knew so many people there. One theory is that ch 16 was actually part of another letter that Paul sent to Ephesus. However, we have no good manuscript evidence for a separate letter (cp. note on 15:33). Perhaps the answer is that Paul was able to greet so many people in Rome because he had encountered them during their travels away from Rome (see Romans Introduction, "Setting," p. 1888).

16:1 *A deacon* (Greek *diakonos,* "servant") refers both to a Christian who is recognized as a servant of Christ and specifically to someone who holds the office of deacon in a particular church (see Phil 1:1; 1 Tim 3:8-12; cp. Acts 6:1-6). • *Cenchrea* was located eight miles from Corinth and functioned as its port. Paul might have been writing this letter to the Romans from Corinth on a winter-long stop there near the end of his third missionary journey (see Acts 20:2-3).

16:2 *she has been helpful to many:* This phrase indicates the ancient role of the patron, a wealthy person who used influence and money to help people and causes (see "Work and Patronage" at 2 Thes 3:6-10, p. 2045). Phoebe was apparently a woman of wealth and influence who used her resources to help missionaries such as Paul.

16:3-16 Although Paul had never visited the Christian community in Rome, he established rapport with these believers by personally greeting many of the church's members. The names reveal that the Roman Christian community was very diverse—Jews and Gentiles, slaves and free, men and women all formed a new society in the church (see Gal 3:26-29).

16:3 *Priscilla and Aquila* were Paul's good friends (see "Priscilla and Aquila" at Acts 18:1-3, p. 1865). After leaving Rome around AD 49, they became his *co-workers* for an extended time in Corinth and Ephesus (see Acts 18–19). They had apparently returned to Rome by the time Paul wrote Romans (about AD 57).

16:5 *the church that meets in their home:* Early Christians did not have large buildings for their meetings—they met in private homes. The church in Rome was composed of a number of house churches where small groups of believers gathered for worship and instruction.

and Junia, my fellow Jews, who were in prison with me. They are highly respected among the apostles and became followers of Christ before I did. ⁸Greet Ampliatus, my dear friend in the Lord. ⁹Greet Urbanus, our co-worker in Christ, and my dear friend Stachys.

¹⁰Greet Apelles, a good man whom Christ approves. And give my greetings to the believers from the household of Aristobulus. ¹¹Greet Herodion, my fellow Jew. Greet the Lord's people from the household of Narcissus. ¹²Give my greetings to Tryphena and Tryphosa, the Lord's workers, and to dear Persis, who has worked so hard for the Lord. ¹³Greet Rufus, whom the Lord picked out to be his very own; and also his dear mother, who has been a mother to me.

¹⁴Give my greetings to Asyncritus, Phlegon, Hermes, Patrobas, Hermas, and the brothers and sisters who meet with them. ¹⁵Give my greetings to Philologus, Julia, Nereus and his sister, and to Olympas and all the believers who meet with them. ¹⁶Greet each other in Christian love. All the churches of Christ send you their greetings.

Closing Remarks and Doxology

¹⁷And now I make one more appeal, my dear brothers and sisters. Watch out for people who cause divisions and upset people's faith by teaching things contrary to what you have been taught. Stay away from them. ¹⁸Such people are not serving Christ our Lord; they are serving their own personal interests. By smooth talk and glowing words they deceive innocent people. ¹⁹But everyone knows that you are obedient to the Lord. This makes me very happy. I want you to be wise in doing right and to stay innocent of any wrong. ²⁰The God of peace will soon crush ᵃSatan under your feet. May the grace of our Lord Jesus be with you.

²¹Timothy, my fellow worker, sends you his greetings, as do Lucius, Jason, and Sosipater, my fellow Jews.

²²I, Tertius, the one writing this letter for Paul, send my greetings, too, as one of the Lord's followers.

²³Gaius says hello to you. He is my host and also serves as host to the whole church. Erastus, the city treasurer, sends you his greetings, and so does our brother Quartus. ²⁵Now all glory to God, who is able to make

16:10
Acts 11:14

16:11
Rom 16:7, 21

16:13
Mark 15:21
2 Jn 1:1

16:16
1 Cor 16:20
1 Thes 5:26
1 Pet 5:14

16:17
1 Cor 5:9, 11
2 Thes 3:6
2 Tim 3:5
Titus 3:10
2 Jn 1:10

16:18
Phil 3:19
Col 2:4
2 Pet 2:3

16:19
Matt 10:16

16:20
Gen 3:15
ᵃsatanas (4567)
▸ 2 Cor 11:14

16:21
Acts 13:1; 16:1; 17:5

16:25
1 Cor 2:1
Eph 1:9; 3:3-5
Col 1:26-27; 2:2
2 Tim 1:9-10
1 Pet 1:20

. . . .

16:7 In Greek, the name *Junia* could refer to a man named *Junias* or to a woman named *Junia*. Most interpreters understand *Junia* as a feminine name. Some late manuscripts accent the word so it reads *Junias*, a masculine name; still others read *Julia* (feminine). This section pairs masculine and feminine names to refer to husband-and-wife teams, so Junia was probably a woman. • *fellow Jews:* Or *compatriots;* also in 16:21. • *who were in prison with me:* When this occurred is uncertain. According to Acts, Paul had been imprisoned overnight in Philippi (Acts 16:19-28); after Romans was written, he would later be imprisoned for two years in Caesarea (Acts 24:27) and for two years in Rome (Acts 28:30-31). Paul was undoubtedly imprisoned on occasions not mentioned in Acts (see 2 Cor 11:23). • *highly respected among the apostles:* This phrase probably indicates that Andronicus and Junia were apostles—i.e., accredited missionaries of the church (see Acts 14:4, 14; 1 Cor 9:5-6; Gal 2:9).

16:10 This *Aristobulus* was probably the same man as the brother of Herod Agrippa I; Aristobulus was a member of the Roman aristocracy who lived in Rome many years prior to his death in AD 48 or 49 (see Josephus, *Antiquities* 18.8.4; *War* 2.11.6). His *household* probably refers to his family and their servants in Rome.

16:11 *fellow Jew:* Or *compatriot.*

16:13 This *Rufus* might be the individual mentioned as the son of Simon of Cyrene, who carried Christ's cross (see Mark 15:21).

16:14 *brothers and sisters:* Literally *brothers;* also in 16:17. See note on 1:13.

16:15 *all the believers:* Literally *all of God's holy people.*

16:16 *in Christian love* (literally *with a sacred kiss*): The kiss was a common way to *greet* another person in the ancient world and particularly among the Jews. It is mentioned frequently in the NT as a greeting (1 Cor 16:20; 2 Cor 13:12; 1 Thes 5:26; see 1 Pet 5:14); the kiss of peace became a standard feature of the Christian liturgy by the second century.

16:17 *people who cause divisions:* Paul had trouble with divisive false teachers elsewhere (see Galatians, Colossians, 1 Timothy), so he warned the Roman church about this danger.

16:20 *The God of peace will soon crush Satan under your feet:* Paul alludes to the curse that God pronounced upon the serpent after he had deceived Adam and Eve in the Garden of Eden (Gen 3:15). Christ, the offspring of Eve, will soon crush Satan under the feet of the church (cp. Matt 16:18-19). • *Lord Jesus:* Some manuscripts read *Lord Jesus Christ.*

16:21 *Timothy* was one of Paul's closest ministry associates (see "Timothy" at

Acts 16:1-3, p. 1860). Timothy accompanied Paul on his second missionary journey (Acts 16:2-3) and was with Paul in Corinth while Paul wrote this letter to the Roman church (see Acts 20:2-4).

16:22 *Tertius* was the scribe (or *amanuensis*) who wrote the letter as Paul dictated. Most ancient letter writers employed such a scribe.

16:23 Some manuscripts add v 24, *May the grace of our Lord Jesus Christ be with you all. Amen.* Still others add this sentence after v 27.• This *Erastus* was probably the individual Paul sent from Ephesus to Macedonia during his third missionary journey (Acts 19:21-22; see 2 Tim 4:20). An inscription in Corinth mentions an Erastus who was a city magistrate, possibly the same Erastus mentioned here.

16:25-27 This doxology makes a very appropriate conclusion to Paul's letter and its argument, reprising many of the themes found at the very beginning (1:1-15). • The doxology is missing in two late manuscripts and is in different places in other manuscripts (after 14:23 and after 15:33). Therefore, these verses might have been added to Paul's letter at a later time. However, the majority of manuscripts do include the doxology at the end of the letter, and it uses vocabulary and themes common in the rest of the letter. Paul most likely wrote it himself as a conclusion to the letter.

ᵇ*apokalupsis* (0602)
▸ 1 Cor 1:7

16:26
Rom 1:2, 5

16:27
Rom 11:36

you strong, just as my Good News says. This message about Jesus Christ has ᵇrevealed his plan for you Gentiles, a plan kept secret from the beginning of time. ²⁶But now as the prophets foretold and as the eternal God has commanded, this message is made known to all Gentiles everywhere, so that they too might believe and obey him. ²⁷All glory to the only wise God, through Jesus Christ, forever. Amen.

16:25 *plan* (literally *mystery*): For Paul, the *mystery* is the truth about God and his plan that was not clearly known in the OT era but which has been revealed in the NT era. While the OT predicted the conversion of Gentiles, it did not make clear that Gentiles would become equal members of the people of God without becoming proselytes of Judaism.

16:26 *the prophets:* Literally *the pro-phetic writings.* • *so that they too might believe and obey him:* Paul uses the same language about the mission to the Gentiles that he used in 1:5, creating a beautiful frame around the letter as a whole.

INTRODUCTION TO THE
NEW LIVING TRANSLATION

*Translation Philosophy
and Methodology*
English Bible translations tend to be governed by one of two general translation theories. The first theory has been called "formal-equivalence," "literal," or "word-for-word" translation. According to this theory, the translator attempts to render each word of the original language into English and seeks to preserve the original syntax and sentence structure as much as possible in translation. The second theory has been called "dynamic-equivalence," "functional-equivalence," or "thought-for-thought" translation. The goal of this translation theory is to produce in English the closest natural equivalent of the message expressed by the original-language text, both in meaning and in style.

Both of these translation theories have their strengths. A formal-equivalence translation preserves aspects of the original text—including ancient idioms, term consistency, and original-language syntax—that are valuable for scholars and professional study. It allows a reader to trace formal elements of the original-language text through the English translation. A dynamic-equivalence translation, on the other hand, focuses on translating the message of the original-language text. It ensures that the meaning of the text is readily apparent to the contemporary reader. This allows the message to come through with immediacy, without requiring the reader to struggle with foreign idioms and awkward syntax. It also facilitates serious study of the text's message and clarity in both devotional and public reading.

The pure application of either of these translation philosophies would create translations at oppo-

site ends of the translation spectrum. But in reality, all translations contain a mixture of these two philosophies. A purely formal-equivalence translation would be unintelligible in English, and a purely dynamic-equivalence translation would risk being unfaithful to the original. That is why translations shaped by dynamic-equivalence theory are usually quite literal when the original text is relatively clear, and the translations shaped by formal-equivalence theory are sometimes quite dynamic when the original text is obscure.

The translators of the New Living Translation set out to render the message of the original texts of Scripture into clear, contemporary English. As they did so, they kept the concerns of both formal-equivalence and dynamic-equivalence in mind. On the one hand, they translated as simply and literally as possible when that approach yielded an accurate, clear, and natural English text. Many words and phrases were rendered literally and consistently into English, preserving essential literary and rhetorical devices, ancient metaphors, and word choices that give structure to the text and provide echoes of meaning from one passage to the next.

On the other hand, the translators rendered the message more dynamically when the literal rendering was hard to understand, was misleading, or yielded archaic or foreign wording. They clarified difficult metaphors and terms to aid in the reader's understanding. The translators first struggled with the meaning of the words and phrases in the ancient context; then they rendered the message into clear, natural English. Their goal was to be both faithful to the ancient texts

and eminently readable. The result is a translation that is both exegetically accurate and idiomatically powerful.

Translation Process and Team
To produce an accurate translation of the Bible into contemporary English, the translation team needed the skills necessary to enter into the thought patterns of the ancient authors and then to render their ideas, connotations, and effects into clear, contemporary English. To begin this process, qualified biblical scholars were needed to interpret the meaning of the original text and to check it against our base English translation. In order to guard against personal and theological biases, the scholars needed to represent a diverse group of evangelicals who would employ the best exegetical tools. Then to work alongside the scholars, skilled English stylists were needed to shape the text into clear, contemporary English.

With these concerns in mind, the Bible Translation Committee recruited teams of scholars that represented a broad spectrum of denominations, theological perspectives, and backgrounds within the worldwide evangelical community. (These scholars are listed at the end of this introduction.) Each book of the Bible was assigned to three different scholars with proven expertise in the book or group of books to be reviewed. Each of these scholars made a thorough review of a base translation and submitted suggested revisions to the appropriate Senior Translator. The Senior Translator then reviewed and summarized these suggestions and proposed a first-draft revision of the base text. This draft served as the basis for several additional phases of exegetical and stylistic committee review. Then the Bible Translation Committee jointly reviewed and approved every verse of the final translation.

Throughout the translation and editing process, the Senior Translators and their scholar teams were given a chance to review the editing done by the team of stylists. This ensured that exegetical errors would not be introduced late in the process and that the entire Bible Translation Committee was happy with the final result. By choosing a team of qualified scholars and skilled stylists and by setting up a process that allowed their interaction throughout the process, the New Living Translation has been refined to preserve the essential formal elements of the original biblical texts, while also creating a clear, understandable English text.

The New Living Translation was first published in 1996. Shortly after its initial publication, the Bible Translation Committee began a process of further committee review and translation refinement. The purpose of this continued revision was to increase the level of precision without sacrificing the text's easy-to-understand quality. This second-edition text was completed in 2004, and an additional update with minor changes was subsequently introduced in 2007. This printing of the New Living Translation reflects the updated 2007 text.

Written to Be Read Aloud
It is evident in Scripture that the biblical documents were written to be read aloud, often in public worship (see Nehemiah 8; Luke 4:16-20; 1 Timothy 4:13; Revelation 1:3). It is still the case today that more people will hear the Bible read aloud in church than are likely to read it for themselves. Therefore, a new translation must communicate with clarity and power when it is read publicly. Clarity was a primary goal for the NLT translators, not only to facilitate private reading and understanding, but also to ensure that it would be excellent for public reading and make an immediate and powerful impact on any listener.

The Texts behind the
New Living Translation
The Old Testament translators used the Masoretic Text of the Hebrew Bible as represented in *Biblia Hebraica Stuttgartensia* (1977), with its extensive system of textual notes; this is an update of Rudolf Kittel's *Biblia Hebraica* (Stuttgart, 1937). The translators also further compared the Dead Sea Scrolls, the Septuagint and other Greek manuscripts, the Samaritan Pentateuch, the Syriac Peshitta, the Latin Vulgate, and any other versions or manuscripts that shed light on the meaning of difficult passages.

The New Testament translators used the two standard editions of the Greek New Testament: the *Greek New Testament*, published by the United Bible Societies (UBS, fourth revised edition, 1993), and *Novum Testamentum Graece*, edited by Nestle and Aland (NA, twenty-seventh edition, 1993). These two editions, which have the same text but differ in punctuation and textual notes, represent, for the most part, the best in modern textual scholarship. However, in cases where strong textual or other scholarly evidence supported the decision, the translators sometimes chose to differ from the UBS and NA Greek texts and followed variant readings found in other ancient witnesses. Significant textual variants of this sort are always noted in the textual notes of the New Living Translation.

Translation Issues
The translators have made a conscious effort to provide a text that can be easily understood by the typical reader of modern English. To this end, we sought to use only vocabulary and language structures in common use today. We avoided using language likely to become quickly dated or that reflects only a narrow subdialect of English, with the goal of making the New Living Translation as broadly useful and timeless as possible.

But our concern for readability goes beyond the concerns of vocabulary and sentence structure. We are also concerned about historical and cultural barriers to understanding the Bible, and we have sought to translate terms shrouded in history and culture in ways that can be immediately understood. To this end:

- We have converted ancient weights and measures (for example, "ephah" [a unit of dry volume] or "cubit" [a unit of length]) to modern English (American) equivalents, since the ancient measures are not generally meaningful to today's readers. Then in the textual footnotes we offer the literal Hebrew, Aramaic, or Greek measures, along with modern metric equivalents.

- Instead of translating ancient currency values literally, we have expressed them in common terms that communicate the message. For example, in the Old Testament, "ten shekels of silver" becomes "ten pieces of silver" to convey the intended message. In the New Testament, we have often translated the "denarius" as "the normal daily wage" to facilitate understanding. Then a footnote offers: "Greek *a denarius*, the payment for a full day's wage." In general, we give a clear English rendering and then state the literal Hebrew, Aramaic, or Greek in a textual footnote.

- Since the names of Hebrew months are unknown to most contemporary readers, and since the Hebrew lunar calendar fluctuates from year to year in relation to the solar calendar used today, we have looked for clear ways to communicate the time of year the Hebrew months (such as Abib) refer to. When an expanded or interpretive rendering is given in the text, a textual note gives the literal rendering. Where it is possible to define a specific ancient date in terms of our modern calendar, we use modern dates in the text. A textual footnote then gives the literal Hebrew date and states the rationale for our rendering. For example, Ezra 6:15 pinpoints the date when the postexilic Temple was completed in Jerusalem: "the third day of the month Adar." This was during the sixth year of King Darius's reign (that is, 515 B.C.). We have translated that date as March 12, with a footnote giving the Hebrew and identifying the year as 515 B.C.

- Since ancient references to the time of day differ from our modern methods of denoting time, we have used renderings that are instantly understandable to the modern reader. Accordingly, we have rendered specific times of day by using approximate equivalents in terms of our common "o'clock" system. On occasion, translations such as "at dawn the next morning" or "as the sun was setting" have been used when the biblical reference is more general.

- When the meaning of a proper name (or a wordplay inherent in a proper name) is relevant to the message of the text, its meaning is often illuminated with a textual footnote. For example, in Exodus 2:10 the text reads: "The princess named him Moses, for she explained, 'I lifted him out of the water.' " The accompanying footnote reads: "*Moses* sounds like a Hebrew term that means 'to lift out.' "

Sometimes, when the actual meaning of a name is clear, that meaning is included in parentheses within the text itself. For example, the text at Genesis 16:11 reads: "You are to name him Ishmael *(which means 'God hears')*, for the LORD has heard your cry of distress." Since the original hearers and readers would have instantly understood the meaning of the name "Ishmael," we have provided modern readers with the same information so they can experience the text in a similar way.

- Many words and phrases carry a great deal of cultural meaning that was obvious to the original readers but needs explanation in our own culture. For example, the phrase "they beat their breasts" (Luke 23:48) in ancient times meant that people were very upset, often in mourning. In our translation we chose to translate this phrase dynamically for clarity: "They went home *in deep sorrow.*" Then we included a footnote with the literal Greek, which reads: "Greek *went home beating their breasts.*" In other similar cases, however, we have sometimes chosen to illuminate the existing literal expression to make it immediately understandable. For example, here we might have expanded the literal Greek phrase to read: "They went home beating their breasts *in sorrow.*" If we had done this,

we would not have included a textual footnote, since the literal Greek clearly appears in translation.

- Metaphorical language is sometimes difficult for contemporary readers to understand, so at times we have chosen to translate or illuminate the meaning of a metaphor. For example, the ancient poet writes, "Your neck is *like* the tower of David" (Song of Songs 4:4). We have rendered it "Your neck is *as beautiful as* the tower of David" to clarify the intended positive meaning of the simile. Another example comes in Ecclesiastes 12:3, which can be literally rendered: "Remember him . . . when the grinding women cease because they are few, and the women who look through the windows see dimly." We have rendered it: "Remember him before your teeth—your few remaining servants—stop grinding; and before your eyes—the women looking through the windows— see dimly." We clarified such metaphors only when we believed a typical reader might be confused by the literal text.

- When the content of the original language text is poetic in character, we have rendered it in English poetic form. We sought to break lines in ways that clarify and highlight the relationships between phrases of the text. Hebrew poetry often uses parallelism, a literary form where a second phrase (or in some instances a third or fourth) echoes the initial phrase in some way. In Hebrew parallelism, the subsequent parallel phrases continue, while also furthering and sharpening, the thought expressed in the initial line or phrase. Whenever possible, we sought to represent these parallel phrases in natural poetic English.

- The Greek term *hoi Ioudaioi* is literally translated "the Jews" in many English translations. In the Gospel of John, however, this term doesn't always refer to the Jewish people generally. In some contexts, it refers more particularly to the Jewish religious leaders. We have attempted to capture the meaning in these different contexts by using terms such as "the people" (with a

footnote: Greek *the Jewish people*) or "the religious leaders," where appropriate.

- One challenge we faced was how to translate accurately the ancient biblical text that was originally written in a context where male-oriented terms were used to refer to humanity generally. We needed to respect the nature of the ancient context while also trying to make the translation clear to a modern audience that tends to read male-oriented language as applying only to males. Often the original text, though using masculine nouns and pronouns, clearly intends that the message be applied to both men and women. A typical example is found in the New Testament letters, where the believers are called "brothers" (*adelphoi*). Yet it is clear from the content of these letters that they were addressed to all the believers— male and female. Thus, we have usually translated this Greek word as "brothers and sisters" in order to represent the historical situation more accurately.

We have also been sensitive to passages where the text applies generally to human beings or to the human condition. In some instances we have used plural pronouns (they, them) in place of the masculine singular (he, him). For example, a traditional rendering of Proverbs 22:6 is: "Train up a child in the way he should go, and when he is old he will not turn from it." We have rendered it: "Direct your children onto the right path, and when they are older, they will not leave it." At times, we have also replaced third person pronouns with the second person to ensure clarity. A traditional rendering of Proverbs 26:27 is: "He who digs a pit will fall into it, and he who rolls a stone, it will come back on him." We have rendered it: "If you set a trap for others, you will get caught in it yourself. If you roll a boulder down on others, it will crush you instead."

We should emphasize, however, that all masculine nouns and pronouns used to represent God (for example, "Father") have been maintained without exception. All decisions of this kind have been driven by the concern to reflect accurately the intended meaning of the original texts of Scripture.

Lexical Consistency in Terminology
For the sake of clarity, we have translated certain original-language terms consistently, especially within synoptic passages and for commonly repeated rhetorical phrases, and within certain word categories such as divine names and non-theological technical terminology (e.g., liturgical, legal, cultural, zoological, and botanical terms). For theological terms, we have allowed a greater semantic range of acceptable English words or phrases for a single Hebrew or Greek word. We have avoided some theological terms that are not readily understood by many modern readers. For example, we avoided using words such as "justification" and "sanctification," which are carryovers from Latin translations. In place of these words, we have provided renderings such as "made right with God" and "made holy."

The Spelling of Proper Names
Many individuals in the Bible, especially the Old Testament, are known by more than one name (e.g., Uzziah/Azariah). For the sake of clarity, we have tried to use a single spelling for any one individual, footnoting the literal spelling whenever we differ from it. This is especially helpful in delineating the kings of Israel and Judah. King Joash/Jehoash of Israel has been consistently called Jehoash, while King Joash/Jehoash of Judah is called Joash. A similar distinction has been used to distinguish between Joram/Jehoram of Israel and Joram/Jehoram of Judah. All such decisions were made with the goal of clarifying the text for the reader. When the ancient biblical writers clearly had a theological purpose in their choice of a variant name (e.g., Esh-baal/Ishbosheth), the different names have been maintained with an explanatory footnote.

For the names Jacob and Israel, which are used interchangeably for both the individual patriarch and the nation, we generally render it "Israel" when it refers to the nation and "Jacob" when it refers to the individual. When our rendering of the name differs from the underlying Hebrew text, we provide a textual footnote, which includes this explanation: "The names 'Jacob' and 'Israel' are often interchanged throughout the Old Testament, referring sometimes to the individual patriarch and sometimes to the nation."

The Rendering of Divine Names
All appearances of *'el, 'elohim,* or *'eloah* have been translated "God," except where the context demands the translation "god(s)." We have generally rendered the tetragrammaton (*YHWH*) consistently as "the LORD," utilizing a form with small capitals that is common among English translations. This will distinguish it from the name *'adonai,* which we render "Lord." When *'adonai* and *YHWH* appear together, we have rendered it "Sovereign LORD." This also distinguishes *'adonai YHWH* from cases where *YHWH* appears with *'elohim,* which is rendered "LORD God." When *YH* (the short form of *YHWH*) and *YHWH* appear together, we have rendered it "LORD GOD." When *YHWH* appears with the term *tseba'oth,* we have rendered it "LORD of Heaven's Armies" to translate the meaning of the name. In a few cases, we have utilized the transliteration, *Yahweh,* when the personal character of the name is being invoked in contrast to another divine name or the name of some other god (for example, see Exodus 3:15; 6:2-3).

In the New Testament, the Greek word *christos* has been translated as "Messiah" when the context assumes a Jewish audience. When a Gentile audience can be assumed, *christos* has been translated as "Christ." The Greek word *kurios* is consistently translated "Lord," except that it is translated "LORD" wherever the New Testament text explicitly quotes from the Old Testament, and the text there has it in small capitals.

Textual Footnotes
The New Living Translation provides several kinds of textual footnotes, all included within the study notes in this edition:

• When for the sake of clarity the NLT renders a difficult or potentially confusing phrase dynamically, we generally give the literal rendering in a textual footnote. This allows the reader to see the literal source of our dynamic rendering and how our transation relates to other more literal translations. These notes are prefaced with "literally." For example, in Acts 2:42 we translated the literal "breaking of bread" (from the Greek) as "the Lord's Supper" to clarify that this verse refers to the ceremonial practice of the church rather than just an ordinary meal. Then we attached a footnote to "the Lord's Supper," which reads: "Literally *the breaking of bread.*"

• Textual footnotes are also used to show alternative renderings, prefaced with the word "Or." These normally occur for passages where an aspect of the meaning is debated. On occasion, we also provide notes on words or phrases that represent a departure from long-standing tradition. These notes are prefaced with "Traditionally rendered." For example, the footnote to the translation "serious skin disease" at Leviticus 13:2 says: "Traditionally rendered *leprosy.* The Hebrew word used throughout this passage is used to describe various skin diseases."

• When our translators follow a textual variant that differs significantly from our standard Hebrew or Greek texts (listed earlier), we document that difference with a footnote. We also footnote cases when the NLT excludes a passage that is included in the Greek text known as the *Textus Receptus* (and familiar to readers through its translation in the King James Version). In such cases, we offer a translation of the excluded text in a footnote, even though it is generally recognized as a later addition to the Greek text and not part of the original Greek New Testament.

• All Old Testament passages that are quoted in the New Testament are identified by a textual footnote at the New Testament location. When the New Testament clearly quotes from the Greek translation of the Old Testament, and when it differs significantly in wording from the Hebrew text, we also place a textual footnote at the Old Testament location. This note includes a rendering of the Greek version, along with a cross-reference to the New Testament passage(s) where it is cited (for example, see notes on Proverbs 3:12; Psalms 8:2; 53:3).

- Some textual footnotes provide cultural and historical information on places, things, and people in the Bible that are probably obscure to modern readers. Such notes should aid the reader in understanding the message of the text. For example, in Acts 12:1, "King Herod" is named in this translation as "King Herod Agrippa" and is identified in a footnote as being "the nephew of Herod Antipas and a grandson of Herod the Great."

- When the meaning of a proper name (or a wordplay inherent in a proper name) is relevant to the meaning of the text, it is either illuminated with a textual footnote or included within parentheses in the text itself. For example, the footnote concerning the name "Eve" at Genesis

3:20 reads: "*Eve* sounds like a Hebrew term that means 'to give life.' " This wordplay in the Hebrew illuminates the meaning of the text, which goes on to say that Eve "would be the mother of all who live."

Cross-References

There are a number of different cross-referencing tools that appear in New Living Translation Bibles, and they offer different levels of help in this regard. All straight-text Bibles include the standard set of textual footnotes that include cross-references connecting New Testament texts to their related Old Testament sources. (See more on this above.)

Many NLT Bibles include an additional short cross-reference system that sets key cross-references at the end of paragraphs and then marks the associated verses with a cross symbol. This space-efficient system, while not being obtrusive, offers many important key connections between passages. Larger study editions include a full-column cross-reference system. This system allows space for a more comprehensive listing of cross-references.

As we submit this translation for publication, we recognize that any translation of the Scriptures is subject to limitations and imperfections. Anyone who has attempted to communicate the richness of God's Word into another language will realize it is impossible to make a perfect translation. Recognizing these limitations, we sought God's guidance and wisdom throughout this project. Now we pray that he will accept our efforts and use this translation for the benefit of the church and of all people.

We pray that the New Living Translation will overcome some of the barriers of history, culture, and language that have kept people from reading and understanding God's Word. We hope that readers unfamiliar with the Bible will find the words clear and easy to understand and that readers well versed in the Scriptures will gain a fresh perspective. We pray that readers will gain insight and wisdom for living, but most of all that they will meet the God of the Bible and be forever changed by knowing him.

THE BIBLE TRANSLATION
COMMITTEE, *October 2007*

BIBLE TRANSLATION TEAM
Holy Bible, New Living Translation

PENTATEUCH
Daniel I. Block, Senior Translator
Wheaton College

GENESIS
Allen Ross, *Beeson Divinity School, Samford University*
Gordon Wenham, *Trinity Theological College, Bristol*

EXODUS
Robert Bergen, *Hannibal-LaGrange College*
Daniel I. Block, *Wheaton College*
Eugene Carpenter, *Bethel College, Mishawaka, Indiana*

LEVITICUS
David Baker, *Ashland Theological Seminary*
Victor Hamilton, *Asbury College*

Kenneth Mathews, *Beeson Divinity School, Samford University*

NUMBERS
Dale A. Brueggemann, *Assemblies of God Division of Foreign Missions*
R. K. Harrison (deceased), *Wycliffe College*
Paul R. House, *Wheaton College*
Gerald L. Mattingly, *Johnson Bible College*

DEUTERONOMY
J. Gordon McConville, *University of Gloucester*
Eugene H. Merrill, *Dallas Theological Seminary*
John A. Thompson (deceased), *University of Melbourne*

HISTORICAL BOOKS
Barry J. Beitzel, Senior Translator
Trinity Evangelical Divinity School

JOSHUA, JUDGES
Carl E. Armerding, *Schloss Mittersill Study Centre*
Barry J. Beitzel, *Trinity Evangelical Divinity School*
Lawson Stone, *Asbury Theological Seminary*

1 & 2 SAMUEL
Robert Gordon, *Cambridge University*
V. Philips Long, *Regent College*
J. Robert Vannoy, *Biblical Theological Seminary*

1 & 2 KINGS
Bill T. Arnold, *Asbury Theological Seminary*

William H. Barnes, *North Central University*
Frederic W. Bush, *Fuller Theological Seminary*

1 & 2 CHRONICLES
Raymond B. Dillard (deceased), *Westminster Theological Seminary*
David A. Dorsey, *Evangelical School of Theology*
Terry Eves, *Erskine College*

RUTH, EZRA—ESTHER
William C. Williams, *Vanguard University*
H. G. M. Williamson, *Oxford University*

WISDOM BOOKS
Tremper Longman III, Senior Translator
Westmont College

JOB
August Konkel, *Providence Theological Seminary*
Tremper Longman III, *Westmont College*
Al Wolters, *Redeemer College*

PSALMS 1–75
Mark D. Futato, *Reformed Theological Seminary*
Douglas Green, *Westminster Theological Seminary*
Richard Pratt, *Reformed Theological Seminary*

PSALMS 76–150
David M. Howard Jr., *Bethel Theological Seminary*
Raymond C. Ortlund Jr., *Trinity Evangelical Divinity School*
Willem VanGemeren, *Trinity Evangelical Divinity School*

PROVERBS
Ted Hildebrandt, *Gordon College*
Richard Schultz, *Wheaton College*
Raymond C. Van Leeuwen, *Eastern College*

ECCLESIASTES, SONG OF SONGS
Daniel C. Fredericks, *Belhaven College*
David Hubbard (deceased), *Fuller Theological Seminary*
Tremper Longman III, *Westmont College*

PROPHETS
John N. Oswalt, Senior Translator
Wesley Biblical Seminary

ISAIAH
John N. Oswalt, *Wesley Biblical Seminary*
Gary Smith, *Midwestern Baptist Theological Seminary*
John Walton, *Wheaton College*

JEREMIAH, LAMENTATIONS
G. Herbert Livingston, *Asbury Theological Seminary*
Elmer A. Martens, *Mennonite Brethren Biblical Seminary*

EZEKIEL
Daniel I. Block, *Wheaton College*
David H. Engelhard, *Calvin Theological Seminary*
David Thompson, *Asbury Theological Seminary*

DANIEL, HAGGAI—MALACHI
Joyce Baldwin Caine (deceased), *Trinity College, Bristol*
Douglas Gropp, *Catholic University of America*
Roy Hayden, *Oral Roberts School of Theology*
Andrew Hill, *Wheaton College*
Tremper Longman III, *Westmont College*

HOSEA—ZEPHANIAH
Joseph Coleson, *Nazarene Theological Seminary*
Roy Hayden, *Oral Roberts School of Theology*
Andrew Hill, *Wheaton College*
Richard Patterson, *Liberty University*

GOSPELS AND ACTS
Grant R. Osborne, Senior Translator
Trinity Evangelical Divinity School

MATTHEW
Craig Blomberg, *Denver Seminary*
Donald A. Hagner, *Fuller Theological Seminary*
David Turner, *Grand Rapids Baptist Seminary*

MARK
Robert Guelich (deceased), *Fuller Theological Seminary*
George Guthrie, *Union University*
Grant R. Osborne, *Trinity Evangelical Divinity School*

LUKE
Darrell Bock, *Dallas Theological Seminary*
Scot McKnight, *North Park University*
Robert Stein, *The Southern Baptist Theological Seminary*

JOHN
Gary M. Burge, *Wheaton College*
Philip W. Comfort, *Coastal Carolina University*
Marianne Meye Thompson, *Fuller Theological Seminary*

ACTS
D. A. Carson, *Trinity Evangelical Divinity School*
William J. Larkin, *Columbia International University*

Roger Mohrlang, *Whitworth University*

LETTERS AND REVELATION
Norman R. Ericson, Senior Translator
Wheaton College

ROMANS, GALATIANS
Gerald Borchert, *Northern Baptist Theological Seminary*
Douglas J. Moo, *Wheaton College*
Thomas R. Schreiner, *The Southern Baptist Theological Seminary*

1 & 2 CORINTHIANS
Joseph Alexanian, *Trinity International University*
Linda Belleville, *Bethel College, Mishawaka, Indiana*
Douglas A. Oss, *Central Bible College*
Robert Sloan, *Baylor University*

EPHESIANS—PHILEMON
Harold W. Hoehner, *Dallas Theological Seminary*
Moises Silva, *Gordon-Conwell Theological Seminary*
Klyne Snodgrass, *North Park Theological Seminary*

HEBREWS, JAMES, 1 & 2 PETER, JUDE
Peter Davids, *Schloss Mittersill Study Centre*
Norman R. Ericson, *Wheaton College*
William Lane (deceased), *Seattle Pacific University*
J. Ramsey Michaels, *S. W. Missouri State University*

1–3 JOHN, REVELATION
Greg Beale, *Wheaton College*
Robert Mounce, *Whitworth University*
M. Robert Mulholland Jr., *Asbury Theological Seminary*

SPECIAL REVIEWERS
F. F. Bruce (deceased), *University of Manchester*
Kenneth N. Taylor (deceased), *Translator, The Living Bible*

COORDINATING TEAM
Mark D. Taylor, *Director and Chief Stylist*
Ronald A. Beers, *Executive Director and Stylist*
Mark R. Norton, *Managing Editor and O.T. Coordinating Editor*
Philip W. Comfort, *N.T. Coordinating Editor*
Daniel W. Taylor, *Bethel University, Senior Stylist*

CONTRIBUTORS

EDITORS

GENERAL EDITOR
Sean A. Harrison

EXECUTIVE EDITOR
Mark D. Taylor

CONTENT EDITORS
David P. Barrett
G. Patrick LaCosse
Bradley J. Lewis
Henry M. Whitney III
Keith Williams

STYLISTIC EDITOR
Linda Schlafer

COPY EDITORS
Keith Williams, Coordinator
Leanne Roberts, Proofreading
  Coordinator
Paul Adams
Jason Driesbach
Adam Graber
Annette Hayward
Judy Modica
Jonathan Schindler
Caleb Sjogren
Cindy Szponder
Lisa Voth
Matthew Wolf

GENERAL REVIEWERS

GENESIS—DEUTERONOMY
Daniel I. Block

JOSHUA—ESTHER, MAPS
Barry J. Beitzel

JOB—SONG OF SONGS
Tremper Longman III

ISAIAH—MALACHI
John N. Oswalt

MATTHEW—ACTS
Grant R. Osborne

ROMANS—REVELATION
Norman R. Ericson

CONTRIBUTING SCHOLARS

GENESIS
Andrew Schmutzer
Allen P. Ross

EXODUS
John N. Oswalt

LEVITICUS
William C. Williams

NUMBERS
Gerald L. Mattingly

DEUTERONOMY
Eugene H. Merrill

JOSHUA
Joseph Coleson

JUDGES
Carl E. Armerding

RUTH
Joseph Coleson
Sean A. Harrison

1 & 2 SAMUEL
Victor P. Hamilton

1 & 2 KINGS
Richard D. Patterson

1 & 2 CHRONICLES
August Konkel

EZRA, NEHEMIAH, ESTHER
Gary V. Smith

JOB
Dale A. Brueggemann

PSALMS
Willem VanGemeren

PROVERBS
Tremper Longman III

ECCLESIASTES
Sean A. Harrison
Daniel C. Fredericks

SONG OF SONGS
Daniel C. Fredericks
Tremper Longman III

ISAIAH
Willem VanGemeren

JEREMIAH, LAMENTATIONS
G. Herbert Livingston

EZEKIEL
Iain Duguid

DANIEL
Gene Carpenter

HOSEA, JOEL
Owen Dickens

AMOS
William C. Williams

OBADIAH
Carl E. Armerding

JONAH
G. Patrick LaCosse

MICAH
Eugene Carpenter

NAHUM, HABAKKUK, ZEPHANIAH
Richard D. Patterson

HAGGAI, ZECHARIAH, MALACHI
Andrew Hill

MATTHEW
Scot McKnight

MARK
Robert Stein

LUKE
Mark Strauss

JOHN
Gary M. Burge

ACTS
Allison Trites

ROMANS
Douglas J. Moo

1 CORINTHIANS
Roger Mohrlang

2 CORINTHIANS
Ralph P. Martin

GALATIANS
Sean A. Harrison

**EPHESIANS, PHILIPPIANS,
PHILEMON**
Roger Mohrlang

COLOSSIANS
Douglas J. Moo

1 & 2 THESSALONIANS
Gene L. Green

1 & 2 TIMOTHY, TITUS
Jon Laansma

HEBREWS
George Guthrie

JAMES
Norman R. Ericson

1 & 2 PETER, JUDE
Douglas J. Moo

1–3 JOHN
Philip W. Comfort

REVELATION
Gerald Borchert

OLD TESTAMENT PROFILES
Tremper Longman III

NEW TESTAMENT PROFILES
Roger Mohrlang

ARTICLES
Daniel I. Block
Eugene Carpenter
Philip W. Comfort
Iain Duguid
Sean A. Harrison
Tremper Longman III
Douglas J. Moo
Grant R. Osborne

Richard D. Patterson
Daniel H. Williams
William C. Williams

WORD STUDY SYSTEM
James A. Swanson
Keith Williams

SPECIAL REVIEWER
Kenneth N. Taylor (deceased)

BIBLE PUBLISHING TEAM
PUBLISHER
Douglas R. Knox

ASSOCIATE PUBLISHER
Blaine A. Smith

ACQUISITIONS DIRECTOR
Kevin O'Brien

ACQUISITIONS EDITOR
Kim Johnson

OTHER SERVICES
GRAPHIC DESIGNERS
Timothy R. Botts (Interior)
Julie Chen (Cover)

CARTOGRAPHY
David P. Barrett

ILLUSTRATORS
Hugh Claycombe
Luke Daab
Sean A. Harrison

TYPESETTING
Joel Bartlett (The Livingstone
    Corporation)
Gwen Elliott

PROOFREADING
Peachtree Editorial Services

INDEXING
Karen Schmitt
    (Schmitt Indexing)

*Many thanks to all who have had a hand
in the creation of this study Bible,
and most of all to the Lord of heaven and earth,
who gave us his word and Spirit so generously.*